Ten Common Mistakes
Retirees Make

HERE'S TO LIVING
HAPPILY EVER AFTER!

Steven H Mohr

9/18/07

Ten Common Mistakes Retirees Make

Steven H. Morton

iUniverse, Inc.
New York Lincoln Shanghai

Ten Common Mistakes Retirees Make

iUniverse books may be ordered through booksellers or by contacting:

iUniverse
2021 Pine Lake Road, Suite 100
Lincoln, NE 68512
www.iuniverse.com
1-800-Authors (1-800-288-4677)

Because of the dynamic nature of the Internet, any Web addresses or links contained in this book may have changed since publication and may no longer be valid.

The views expressed in this work are solely those of the author and do not necessarily reflect the views of the publisher, and the publisher hereby disclaims any responsibility for them.

ISBN: 978-0-595-45476-1 (pbk)
ISBN: 978-0-595-89788-9 (ebk)

Printed in the United States of America

"Human nature is always in conflict with successful investing."

—Warren Buffett

Contents

1

How Secure Is Your Retirement?

"My biggest fear is that the money I have isn't going to be enough."

The speaker was a gentleman I'll call Bill, a highly successful business owner fifty-seven years of age with a net worth of approximately $2.5 million, excluding his large and beautiful home, his second home, his three cars, and his speedboat.

You might say, "He's in pretty good shape! What's he worried about?"

Yet the fact is that the number one fear facing the affluent is that they'll outlive their money. This fear affects even individuals and couples who have succeeded in their careers and are quite comfortable financially. And Bill's fear of outliving his not inconsiderable wealth prompted this discussion.

Bill had come to my office because he wanted to talk about his retirement, which was only three years away. He had never really focused on financial or retirement planning. He'd spent all of his time building his business and enjoying life.

I asked Bill to tell me what he had in place for retirement. He was a little embarrassed to tell me about the bunch of different things and people that constituted his retirement "plan." One of his golfing buddies, an attorney who specialized in real estate transactions, had done his will. A variable annuity salesman he met at his country club had sold him a policy that he (and probably also the salesman) didn't really understand. He also had a bunch of mutual funds that he bought and sold at the suggestion of some of his investor friends. Bill told me he had the nagging sensation these friends were a lot like people who went to Las Vegas: They only told you about their wins. He certainly didn't seem to have as many "wins" in his portfolio as they claimed for themselves.

I could see the sheepishness in Bill's eyes as he told me more about his investment planning, financial planning, and retirement planning. Bill was a take-charge guy who rarely took a passive attitude toward life, at work or at play. He and his wife, Kathy, had been married for thirty years. The two oldest kids were through college and out of the house. The youngest, a member of the "boomerang generation," had gotten a taste of the real world and made a sharp retreat to a hastily assembled bedroom in the basement of their home. His oldest daughter had already presented him with two grandchildren, and Bill's entire demeanor shifted when he started talking about how much he loved his grandbabies. He stopped looking like a captain of industry with a retirement problem and started looking like the happiest, most tickled individual on the face of the earth.

Bill knew that retirement had changed radically since his parents' day. No longer did you look to your employer to provide you with a pension. Workers simply don't work for the same company for thirty or forty years and retire with a reliable pension. Employees move around more these days and employers have found that the traditional pension plans are simply too expensive to fund.

Bill had gone into business for himself because his father's company had gone out of business two years after Bill's father's retirement, essentially stranding Bill Sr. financially and forcing him to make an undesired return to the working world. Bill swore that the same thing would never happen to him, which is what led him to build his own highly successful enterprise.

Bill also knew that he would have to find more proactive ways to fund retirement, because his post-work life would likely last much longer than that of his father, who worked into his early seventies and died at seventy-four. Bill knew that his life expectancy, and that of his wife—both of whom enjoyed excellent health, although neither were exercise or diet fanatics—would simply last much longer.

Most of Bill's forebears, and Kathy's as well, lived into their eighties and some even their nineties. Now, $2.5 million sounds like a lot of money, until you got to thinking about how many years that money would need to last. It was a sobering thought for Bill. Again, the fear that he and his wife might outlive their savings was the number one reason that had brought him into my office.

There was a second reason for our meeting as well. Bill, a huge basketball fan, loved to quote the great basketball coach John Wooden when it came to describing his philosophy of building his business: "The team that makes the most mistakes wins." Coach Wooden also liked to say, "If you're not making mistakes, then you're not doing anything. I'm positive that a doer makes mistakes."

Yet, as confident as Bill was at the helm of his business, he was extremely doubtful about his choices when it came to his retirement and financial planning. He felt confused by the variety of products available, uncertain as to what he needed or how much, how to make it all work together, and whether those choices would be the best choices. In short, the man who had built his business into a huge success by taking all the appropriate risks and making all the necessary mistakes, found himself in an area where he didn't want to make any mistakes at all.

Bill sensed that a serious misstep with his financial and retirement planning could trigger a seven-figure shortfall, and I had to agree with him. His concerns were well-grounded.

The simple fact is that most people don't want to think about retirement any more than they want to think about their own demise. Retirement for most of us still connotes a sense of being pushed to the side, being unwanted and unneeded, twiddling one's thumbs or playing endless rounds of golf. (And, as some retirees admit, even golf can get old when it's all you do.)

Bill is also not alone. There are millions of individuals in his position—affluent people with seven-figure net worths who have never made the time to focus on their retirement planning. It seems as though thinking about retirement is the one thing that just about everybody agrees we can ignore or defer well into the future. But when retirement becomes not just a hazy concept, but an actual date on the calendar—which most people plan between two to five years out—the situation changes. All of a sudden, those twin demons—"Will what we have be enough?" and "How do I avoid making a seven-figure mistake?"—loom larger and larger.

That's why I was so glad that Bill had come in to talk about his future. I specialize in working with people in just his position—successful individuals who have devoted their entire lives to their careers, families, and communities, but who may not have given a lot of thought as to what their lives will be like when they retire from their current jobs and their "second lives" begin. Such individuals are often highly motivated to get their planning done, and with good reason: The clock is ticking. Making the right decision now—and not making seven-figure mistakes—can have huge ramifications down the road.

What's the Rush?

The challenge about retirement planning is that typically there is no deadline attached to it. Doing your taxes is the complete opposite. You've got a deadline: April 15. (Or, if you want to take an extension, October 15.) The government is standing over you and saying, "Get those taxes done—or else." When it comes to retirement, however, there's nobody standing over you imposing any sort of deadline. As a result, many people devote more time to planning summer vacations than they invest in planning the third—or perhaps even the half—of their lives that follows the day of their retirement.

I've noticed, over my thirty-plus years in the financial services sector, that individuals as intelligent and successful as Bill do tend to repeat certain mistakes when it comes to retirement planning (or lack thereof). I call these the "million-dollar mistakes" because the financial ramifications of these commonplace errors really do have seven-figure price tags attached to them. I've worked with countless individuals and families who came to me either because they had made some of those mistakes or because they simply wanted to find a way to create the ideal retirement scenario for themselves.

I thought it might be a good idea to share what those ten critical mistakes are, and what they're all about. I want to offer you the same guidance I provide my clients on how to avoid those mistakes, along with strategies for taking your retirement into your own hands and approaching it from a proactive standpoint. You'll find one mistake per chapter as we go forward.

If you have a financial position anything like Bill's, then the short time it takes to read this book might just save you a million dollars or more. Even better, it can *earn* you millions of dollars. The security that comes from knowing you have enough in the bank to take care of your financial needs, those of your family, and those of your favorite charitable organizations cannot possibly be overestimated.

Although most might say I'm in the financial or retirement planning field, when it comes right down to it, I'm in the "peace of mind" business. It's my job to show my clients how to avoid those seven-figure pitfalls and turn them into seven-figure paydays. And that's exactly what you'll find in this book.

Who Is This Morton Guy, Anyway?

You might be wondering what qualifies me to write this book. So I'll take just a little bit of time to tell you about how I came to do what I do.

During college, I worked for an accounting firm during my junior and senior years, then took a job with the same firm, based in Denver, after I graduated. My mind was on my work during the weekdays, but I couldn't wait for Friday evening, when I would strap my skis to my car and head through all that traffic for the mountains. If you've ever skied in Colorado, you know exactly what I'm talking about. And if you've ever tried to get through rush hour traffic in Denver on a Friday night, you also know what I'm talking about!

So I figured this would be an ideal time to trade in my city job for one in a small mountain town. Good-bye, traffic! Hello, snow! After a year of hard work on the weekdays and soft powder on the slopes on the weekends, I was made a partner in the firm, which wouldn't have happened nearly as quickly at my old firm in Denver. After five years, we had built the firm to a point where we tripled the business during my time there.

In big cities, an accountant typically specializes in one area or another—individual tax, corporate tax, partnerships, school board audits. But in a small town you end up doing a little of everything. We became so successful, in fact, that there were times that we just simply did not have the capacity to take on new clients—and we would have to shut the door to new business! That tells you the level of success we had achieved—and also gives an idea of the number of hours I was working. Typically, a CPA works seventy-hour weeks during tax season. I was working nearly that many hours every month of the year. The ski slopes were beckoning, but I had little time to hit the powder because I was working so much.

After five years with that firm, I was so burned-out that I turned to the senior partner and said, "I need a month off. I've got to get my head straight."

I'll never forget his response. "I'm the senior partner around here," he reminded me. "If we're going to structure things so that anybody can take a month off, it's going to be *me,* not you."

I was stunned. This was the response I received for helping build this business to its pinnacle of success? How would *you* feel if your partner or boss said that to you?

"I think I've built the wrong business," I replied. "I'm leaving."

And I left.

I didn't leave the business high and dry, of course. By that time, we had worked hard enough to create a position for a third accountant-partner, and I essentially turned over my work to him. It was 1981, I was now six years out of college, and I found myself wondering what I wanted to do with the rest of my life.

Around that time, I had lunch with an individual who had recently gotten certification in what was then a brand-new field. I had never heard the term "financial planning" before, and I asked him to tell me what he did. He explained that he helped people to make investment decisions and planned their financial futures.

Wait a minute, I thought. That's what I do!

A Dollar Here, A Dollar There …

Let me explain. When I was at the small-town accounting firm, we developed a reputation for asking the probing questions that other accountants did not ask. These questions may not seem all that important, but they add up to a lot of money cut from a person's tax bill or add to a person's net worth. For example, we would ask our clients how many miles they drove for charitable endeavors. Most of our clients never realized that they could deduct miles driven for activities that supported their church or the United Way. We would dig for deductions that were perfectly legal but unknown to most of our clientele. The cumulative effect of those legitimate deductions: whopping tax savings for our clients.

At the same time, a new product called the "money market fund"—about as blasé a financial vehicle as you could imagine today—had just come onto the scene. Interest rates back in the early 1980s were very high. When I looked at my clients' income statements on Schedule B of their tax returns, I'd see that they were not earning very much interest. Typically, they were getting 4 ¼ percent on their passbooks. I would suggest that they open up a money market account at 8 percent—and they thought I was the greatest genius that had ever filled out a tax form! It wasn't rocket science. It was very straightforward. It was also something that I just took for granted as a part of my job: minimize tax burdens, maximize net worth.

In that one respect, nothing's really changed in my career.

I realize that this profession of financial planning, so new at the time, could afford me the opportunity to do what I really wanted to do. It would allow me to help people be proactive and plan for the future instead of sort through their boxes of receipts to see what they had done in the past and report it properly on their tax returns, which is more typically the domain of a CPA. At that time, there were no more than 300 certified financial planners in the entire United States. This year, the total number of CFPs is almost 53,000. So I've had the privilege of working in this field practically since its inception twenty-five years ago.

After I was certified as a financial planner, my new career took off. I was able to build a financial planning practice that today has the distinction of having served thousands of individuals. We help them navigate the shoals of retirement planning, help them maximize their retirement income, charitable giving, and gifts to their children and grandchildren. Above all, we help them find financial peace of mind.

Why am I so familiar with the critical mistakes that I'm about to share with you? Because I've been doing this for so long, I've seen so many situations and circumstances that could have been vastly improved if people had known better. Many times, people will seek a financial planner when something is broken. If you don't get anything else out of this book, take away this lesson: Do some comprehensive planning before you take any action. You wouldn't dream of building a house without first having a detailed set of plans prepared by an experienced architect. So why would you want to build your financial future without a proper set of plans?

Make No Mistake …

I am certain that I can spare you the insecurities and inefficiencies that have plagued many of the individuals who have come to me over the past twenty-five years, looking for guidance about their financial futures and their retirement. Nothing would give me greater pleasure than to help you find the most valuable commodity of all: peace of mind. This comes from knowing that you've made the best possible decisions and that your retirement has the maximum likelihood of providing for you and those you love everything that all of you will ever need.

So let's take a look at some of those seven-figure mistakes and together we'll discuss strategies for avoiding them and creating the secure financial future in retirement that you—and your family—so richly deserve.

2

Mistake #10: Paying Too Much Tax

You're retired or approaching retirement age. Which of the following topics would you rather discuss?

Option 1: your grandchildren, your vacation home(s), and your leisure time activities—fishing, skiing, playing golf, etc.?

Option 2: taxes.

This is a pretty easy question. Only an accountant, financial planner, or tax attorney would even consider the latter option. Whenever I introduce the topic of taxes to my clients, I always encounter a very high "MEGO" factor (short for "My Eyes Glaze Over"). And I'm sure that no matter how well-intentioned you are about protecting your own financial future, that last thing you *really* want to do right now is sit down with me and have a discussion about the IRS.

You'd rather tell me about your grandchildren—how smart and cute they are, how much fun they can be. You might even have that guilty feeling that hints at the fact that you enjoy them even more than you enjoy your own children. As the bumper sticker says, "If I had known grandkids would be so much fun, I would have had them first!"

For most older, affluent Americans, talking about vacation homes runs a not-so-distant second to talking about grandchildren. A lot of folks—and I'm one of them—simply feel that few parts of the country provide a year-round climate in which they really thrive. I love North Carolina for spring and fall, but the summer gets a little too hot and humid for my taste, and in the winter, well, you can't beat the skiing in the Rockies. So, like many affluent people, I maintain more than one home, because that's the way I like to live.

What's the Connection (If Any?)?

You might be wondering: What do grandchildren and second homes have to do with taxes? Let me tie in the subject of sensible tax planning with the idea of doing more for and with your grandchildren, *and* enjoying the benefits of a second home while saving on your tax bill. Now, would you give me your attention for just a few pages?

Aha! I thought so!

Retirement is much more complicated today. There's a good chance that your grandfather or great-grandfather was born and died in the same city, and during his lifetime his parents, grandparents, siblings, children, and even grandchildren all resided within a relatively short distance of his home.

Take my own grandfather as an example. He was born in Omaha, Nebraska, and lived there for his entire life. When he began to experience the effects of aging and was no longer able to care for himself to a degree that satisfied him, he didn't move into a retirement community or nursing home. He moved into my parents' bedroom, and my parents moved downstairs, to the basement. And so things remained for a couple of years, until he needed more care than we could provide.

It's a different ball game today. We live in an extraordinarily mobile society. Once kids apply to colleges around the country or start shooting off resumes to employers in distant cities, there is a very strong likelihood that they and their children (your precious grandchildren!) will be living in distant cities for the rest of their lives. This means that for an increasing number of grandparents, it takes more money, time, and effort to visit the grandkids. It's no longer a quick jaunt across town, as it was in my grandfather's day. It takes a lot of money to make frequent trips to see the grandchildren, and this is especially true if you have grandchildren growing up in several different states. Some retirees actually move so that they can be closer to members of their families.

The concern extends beyond staying in touch with far-flung family members. The equally large issue has to do with health care. Back in the day, high-level health care was limited to the major cities of the United States. Rural areas simply could not compete in terms of providing the highest levels of care, and this was especially true for older individuals with serious healthcare needs. In my grandfather's day, mobility was severely restricted, first by societal norms, which did not have retirees traipsing around the country as snowbirds or sunbirds, and also by their need for health care. You had to rely on your family, because the financial resources might not have been available to pay for care, and because even if you could afford it, only those in metropolitan areas had much chance of finding it.

Country Doctors Practicing Big-City Medicine

Today, everything has changed. You can find extremely high-quality health care in just about any part of the country that appeals to affluent Americans. Take Pinehurst, North Carolina, just down the road from where I write these words. In Pinehurst you can find anything in the medical field that in past decades you would have had to visit a major city to discover. This is true whether you are talking about Jackson Hole, Wyoming; Sun Valley, Idaho; Palm Beach, Florida; or any locale equally attractive to the affluent and the medical practitioners who serve them.

In short, travel—and the possibility of relocating—is very much a reality for older Americans as never before. They want to get on the road to see their grandchildren, they have the financial wherewithal to enjoy all of life's experiences, from downhill skiing to water sports to whatever tickles their fancy, and they no longer rely on immediate family to meet their health care needs. The affluent are on the go.

Believe it or not, there is a great tax-planning opportunity here, since all states do not tax income at the same rate. In fact, there are several states that have no income tax at all. For example, many people enjoy Florida for most of the year, but it gets too darn hot during the summer months. Many of them retreat to their second homes in the mountains of North Carolina. For income tax purposes, they want to claim Florida as home since there is no state income tax there. Most of your income is taxed in your resident state, so you need to be very careful about where to claim your residence. There are several issues the taxing authorities examine that help you show your intended residence. While these issues are outside the scope of this book, be sure to get some help on how to go about this in the right way.

The Wrong Way vs. The Roth Way

Wouldn't it be nice if you could get Uncle Sam to help underwrite the cost of your travel?

All too many retirees end up spending huge sums of money and even cheating themselves out of some of life's greatest experiences—with and without grandchildren—simply because they do not know how to shift their tax strategies in retirement.

Let me give you an example. Not long ago, I was having a first meeting with a new client we'll call Jack. I asked Jack how much income tax he paid the previous year, his first year in retirement.

"Practically nothing!" he replied triumphantly.

I shook my head sadly. "I'm so sorry to hear that," I said.

That got Jack's attention.

"What are you talking about?" he asked, greatly surprised. "Isn't the whole idea to save all the money you can on taxes?"

"Not necessarily." I want to share with you the explanation that I gave Jack.

Sometimes, it pays to pay a little bit in taxes so that you can keep—or pass on to your heirs—a lot more. Think for a moment about the graduated income tax system we have in this country. Right now, you pay 10 percent on the first chunk of your taxable income, 15 percent of the next chunk, 25 percent of the chunk after that, and all the way up to 35 percent, the current maximum federal tax burden for couples making more than $336,550 a year. Most of us, when we think about taxes, look at our tax burdens as a straightforward, simple percentage of our entire income for the year. In other words, we look at the average amount that we are paying in taxes instead of looking at how much we are paying at each percent milestone. And therein lies Jack's mistake.

Jack did not take advantage of the opportunity to declare income and pay tax on that income at those relatively low levels of 10 to 25 percent. Now, you might be wondering why Jack would want to pay any more tax than he had to.

Jack has about $2 million in his IRA, which rolled over from his company's pension plan. Anytime Jack makes a withdrawal from that IRA, he must declare and pay income tax on the amount of his withdrawal. Since he knew this was the case, he instead chose to live on the tax-free income from municipal bonds, and the only tax he had to pay was some capital gains tax on some stocks he sold. It sounds like a good strategy, but here's an even better one, and if you watch carefully, you'll see how it can benefit not just Jack (or you), but the grandchildren as well.

Let's say Jack took $100,000 from his IRA and put that money into a Roth IRA. You see, you can convert a portion of your IRA to a Roth IRA and all you have to do is meet the qualifications as to maximum income ($100,000 or less) to do it. This maximum income does not include the conversion amount. Remember that as a retiree, you have a degree of control over your taxable income that you didn't have while you were working. Yes, Jack would have to pay income tax on that $100,000. But he wouldn't have to pay much tax compared to his old tax bracket when he was enjoying his high income. Some of the conversion would be taxed at 10 percent, some at 15 percent, some at 25. So Jack would have a tax bill for that $100,000 of approximately $18,000.

What does Jack get for that money? Well, a Roth IRA has many significant advantages over a traditional IRA. First, a Roth IRA does not require mandatory withdrawals, as does a regular IRA. The government does not want you to use traditional IRAs as an estate-planning device. So, in their collective wisdom, they decreed that once you reach the age of seventy and a half, you must withdraw money from your IRA every year, and, not so incidentally, pay income tax on that money. How much do you have to withdraw each year? It depends on how old you are. With a Roth IRA, however, there is no requirement to withdraw money. Instead, you can take that $100,000 Roth IRA and pass it on to a grandchild. Distributions from Roth IRAs are income tax-free. This is true whether it's yours or your heir's.

Now, you might be saying, "I could just leave my grandchild that same amount in my will. Why do I have to go through all that business of moving money from a regular IRA into a Roth IRA, and why would I want to pay that tax?"

The answer has to do with the benefits to your granddaughter, the beneficiary of the Roth IRA. Let's name her Sarah and say that she'll be twenty-four years old at the time she receives your gift of the Roth IRA. If that money is invested at a rate of 8 percent, that Roth IRA through minimum distributions will provide Sarah, over the next fifty years of her life, a whopping $1.5 million—*and every penny of it is tax-free*. This assumes she doesn't reinvest it. If she does, Sarah would accumulate even more.

If you simply leave the money in your estate it certainly will not have the tax-favored status that money in a Roth IRA enjoys. For a mere $18,000 in income tax now, you can create a wealth vehicle for your granddaughter that will serve her throughout her entire life. (And if she receives the money at twenty-four, she may not be ready for it. Would you have been?)

This is one illustration of how a little bit of tax planning—and even the willingness to take a relatively small tax hit now—can have wonderful implications for you and your family down the road. So making the supreme goal of your tax planning the reduction of current taxes, which so many financial planners and their clients do, really can be considered a major mistake.

Just the Tax, Ma'am

A second concern about taxes that ties in neatly with the question of grandchildren, mobility, and second homes has to do with where we choose to live. Now, I love skiing, as you know, so my first thought would be to own a second home in Colorado. If I had grandchildren in Colorado, it would be even more of an imperative for me to live or have my second home there. Few retirees take into consideration whether the states in which they maintain their second homes are high-tax, low-tax, or no-tax states.

For example, Wyoming, Nevada, and Florida have no state income tax. North Carolina does—a relatively high 8 percent. (California's is even higher, at 10 percent, but we won't even get into that now.) If I love skiing, wouldn't it make sense for me to consider having a second home in Wyoming, a relatively short and easy trip to tax-happy North Carolina?

The tax savings are substantial. You might say, "What's the difference if I'm just paying an extra 8 percent on my taxes?" It's a fair question, but consider this: Most states do not differentiate between capital gains and ordinary income; they take the same percentage of either one. Many retirees have substantial capital gains. While the federal government taxes capital gains at a lower rate than ordinary income, states don't make that distinction. So a retiree in Wyoming with the same capital gains as a retiree in North Carolina will be saving a considerable amount of money.

It's not inconceivable that the amount of money saved by maintaining a second residence in a no-tax state will be enough money to pay for that second residence. In other words, if you pick the right state based on its proximity to your grandchildren, its availability of leisure time activities that you like, and whether or not it has a state income tax, you can save yourself a small fortune. Smart retirees know and do this. That's a second strategy for getting Uncle Sam to help you spend more time with those grandkids you love so much. (Okay, and their parents, too.)

Too Many Bonds?

Let me share a third strategy that many retirees fail to employ. Let's say that your portfolio is heavy in bonds, which is often the case for the older and affluent. There's a good chance that you are in municipal bonds, which might pay 3 1/2 percent tax-free. Corporate bonds might pay a higher rate—let's say 5 percent—but after you subtract the 40 percent tax bite, your net earnings are 3 percent. If you are in a high tax bracket, as are most affluent working people, then municipal bonds make a lot of sense. But what happens after you retire?

It may well be that you can come out ahead with corporate bonds compared with municipal bonds once you find yourself in a lower, post-retirement tax rate. Yet most retirees fail to examine their bond holdings in light of the new level of taxes they are paying. It's a slightly harder stretch for me to connect this concept with grandkids and second homes, but the more money you save on your income tax, the more time you can spend with your precious grandchildren, doing whatever you both love most.

I could offer more examples, but I think the point is clear. Tax strategy in retirement isn't simply about paying the least amount of tax. Instead, it's about considering your income tax strategy within the context of everything else that's important in life—where you want to live, how you want to live, and what you want to do with your new, ample leisure time—and those with whom you want to spend it.

3

Mistake #9: Leaving Social Security Money on the Table

Don't look now, but the generation that grew up not trusting anyone over thirty is ready for their Social Security benefits.

But is the Social Security system ready for the baby boomers?

Probably not.

Imagine if there had never been a Social Security system in the United States, and that the government had found a better way to provide a safety net for the indigent, disabled, and aged. Without an expensive Social Security Administration to maintain and without those decades of ill-conceived investing and spending, that money would have been yours to invest all this time. If you're age sixty-two and you've been contributing the maximum amount of Social Security tax each year, just in the last twenty-five years, you have waved good-bye to $128,465. If you're self-employed, your contribution was close to double that amount: $246,108. (Employers today contribute the same amount to Social Security as employees, so either way, nearly a quarter-million dollars' worth of money that could have been your compensation went to Uncle Sam.)

But money is never stagnant—it either grows or diminishes with time. So if you figure in inflation, in 2007 dollars, the total Social Security bite over the last twenty-five years is $161,343. Unfortunately, it gets worse. If you had just taken that same amount in interest-bearing CDs, you would have accumulated $219,364.

If you'd stuck that same amount of money in municipal bonds, you would be looking at a nest egg of $284,054.

If you had put that same amount into commercial real estate, your net worth would be increased to the magnificent tune of $300,216.

If you'd put it in the stock market, doing nothing more sophisticated than buying the Dow Jones Industrial Average for the past twenty-five years, you'd be sitting pretty with $558,769.

If there had never been a Social Security Administration, and if our generation had been allowed to keep that money and invest it, the capital gains taxes on those investments would almost certainly be enough to wipe out the entire federal deficit!

But, sad to say, that's not how things worked out. Every year, like a good citizen, you paid your Social Security tax, and all you got was the now-illusory promise that when you retired, you'd be able to draw from that Social Security Trust Fund to supplement the costs of your own post-retirement life. As we all know, however, there is no great big pile of money sitting in a Washington bank vault labeled "Social Security Trust Fund."

Instead, the Social Security Administration lent that money to itself. It took your hard-earned salary and lent it to the general fund of the federal government, which frittered it away as only a federal government can. All the government has to show for that river of cash is a pile of IOUs, in the form of treasury notes. It's a safe investment, but not an especially lucrative one. In fact, the government could hardly have made an investment choice that would have guaranteed a lower rate of return.

The Future of Social Security

Will the money be there when you need it? According to the Social Security Trustees Report of May 2006, Social Security tax revenues will equal Social Security tax outlays by 2017, just a decade from now. Analysts predict that the Social Security Trust Fund will actually go broke by the year 2040. (A year ago, they thought it wouldn't happen until 2041, so the end is indeed getting nearer.) Social Security is currently underfunded to the tune of $4.6 *trillion*, which means that within a few short decades, those Americans who failed to save money during their working lives will be in deep trouble.

There's no longer any doubt that the Social Security system is headed for disaster. The only debate is how long it will be before the crisis hits. The problem is that too few workers are supporting too many retirees, and the problem will only become exacerbated as increasing numbers of baby boomers end their careers and start collecting Social Security.

On top of that, the Social Security system has developed responsibilities far beyond anything that President Franklin D. Roosevelt envisioned when he created the plan. Back then, Social Security was simply intended to supplement the income of Americans who were struggling through the Depression. It was never meant as a universal safety net for families or for the disabled, and it was never intended to serve as the primary source of retirement income for the working class and even much of the middle class. And yet, that's what it's turned into. And with increasing demands chasing less and less money, it is our generation that will find itself unable to collect on the promise that Social Security made us: that if we work hard and support the system, one day the system will support us.

This probably hits much harder for individuals and families further down the socioeconomic scale than the average reader of this book. For them, the collapse of the Social Security system represents the collapse of much, if not all, of their retirement funds. For an individual who has been financially successful, it means the potential loss of up to $25,000 a year in benefits.

Maximum Security

It's critically important for members of our generation to set aside our sense of dismay over the government's actions. Instead, we must determine how best to maximize our own benefits under the Social Security system as we know it now and as it may evolve in the future. The key question is when to make the election to start taking benefits. You can only make this decision once and you cannot unmake and remake it, so it's imperative that you get it right. If you're going to be retiring on an income in the low six figures or more, as is the case for many readers of this book, the extra $25,000 in annual income that Social Security represents won't make or break you. Still, it's real money and it's yours, so you might as well maximize what you get.

However, when you should elect to start taking benefits isn't clear-cut, not by a long shot. There are many variables, many of which are unknown to most accountants and attorneys, who therefore are unable to give the best advice to their clients. I'd like to share with you a "decision tree" so that you can choose the wisest course for yourself.

SOCIAL SECURITY BENEFITS DECISION TREE

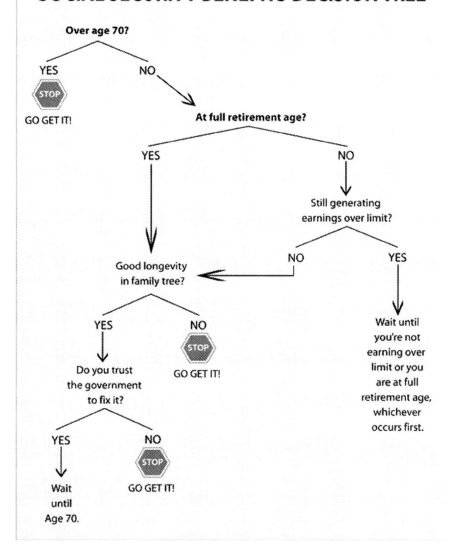

The main point to keep in mind about the rules of Social Security is that they're in constant flux, and it's only going to get worse for people at our socioeconomic level. The partial taxation of Social Security benefits is, in my opinion, only the first step in reducing or perhaps even eliminating Social Security benefits for the wealthy. So one of the key factors in your decision about when to elect to receive benefits has to do with your optimism about the government's ability to solve the Social Security mess and your feelings about whether they will attempt to do so by "sticking it to the rich."

The Basics of Security

Let's first get a few basic concepts on the table. You can begin to take Social Security benefits at age sixty-two. If you do, you will get a smaller amount—three-quarters of 1 percent per month below "normal retirement age." In other words, the government has an arbitrary "normal retirement age" (also known as "full retirement age") that it sets. It used to be sixty-five; as of this writing, it's sixty-five years and eight months. Before long, it will increase to sixty-five years and ten months and it will keep increasing. The more they inflate that figure, the fewer beneficiaries to whom they must pay 100 percent of their Social Security benefits.

So your first option is to start taking Social Security at age sixty-two, although you will pay a penalty via a smaller amount. That penalty is determined on a sliding scale based on age. Your second option is to wait for the "normal retirement age," which, as we just saw, is a moving target. Your third option is to wait even longer, because the longer you wait, the higher your Social Security checks will be.

So how do you decide what to do? Let's take a look at some of the typical situations in which members of our generation find themselves.

Let's start with the individual who is sixty-two years old. If you are still working, you may be wise to wait. That's because, if you're still working, the government reduces your benefits by $1 for every $2 over a very low income threshold. In other words, the government figures that as long as you're out there in the trenches, you don't need that much help because you're still making money. So they have a formula for reducing your Social

Security benefits even further. Again, if you're still working, you might as well wait, because you're just going to give it back due to that reduction system.

If you're sixty-two and you've already retired, the two key factors to consider are your expectations about longevity and your optimism that the government will finally figure this whole Social Security thing out. Some people come to me and say, "Nobody in my family ever made it to seventy. I probably won't live that long, so I might as well elect to get Social Security benefits now." Keep in mind that longevity is only one factor in determining how well a person ages. There's diet, exercise, lifestyle choices, and the rest. But if you're convinced that you're not going to live all that long, you might as well start taking your Social Security benefits.

By contrast, if your relatives typically live into their late eighties or even nineties, then you may want to wait. The longer you wait, the higher your check will be. While this is common knowledge, most people don't realize that you typically have to live to eighty-five in order to equal the benefits you give up by not electing for Social Security sooner. If you think you're going to live into your late eighties or even your nineties, then it certainly makes sense to wait until at least your normal retirement age before you start collecting.

The next issue is optimism. If you think the government is going to figure out a way to get Social Security back on track without penalizing its wealthiest recipients, then you may elect to wait a little longer. But if you retain a strong sense of mistrust, take the money and run.

The next age threshold is your "normal retirement age," which, as we saw, continues to change. The government thinks that the younger you are, the longer you should wait before you reach this milestone. Thus, that level changes every year in order to keep the system from going broke sooner. Once you reach your "natural retirement age," whatever it is based on the year of your birth, you are entitled to receive your full Social Security benefit. It doesn't mean you're going to get to keep the whole thing, as up to 85 percent of your benefit is taxable. If you've reached this age, there are a few key factors to consider as you make your decision of when to elect.

If you're between sixty-five and sixty-nine, I would call you a "young retiree." It's relatively easy for you to get around. This is the generation of retirees who travel more and who still have expensive hobbies—skiing, fly-fishing in exotic locations, and the like. This generation has a greater need for cash. If you're in that band, you may elect to take Social Security now, so you've got that extra chunk of cash coming in every month. To the extent that you wait to begin benefits after your normal retirement age, your benefit will increase on a sliding scale. Once you turn seventy, your benefit no longer increases, so you should start taking it at this age at the latest. If you ignore this rule, you're just leaving money on the table.

In short, the question you want to ask yourself is whether you need the cash now, and whether you think the cash will be there down the road.

The Marriage Penalty ... on Geritol

Like most Americans, I would be thrilled if the United States government could get its act together with regard to the Social Security crisis. I've got a personal reason as well. My father has a girlfriend whom he would love to marry, and she would love to marry him. The only problem is that the Social Security system, in its wisdom, has ruled that when your spouse dies, you get their Social Security benefits—but only if you do not remarry. In other words, if my father and his girlfriend were to get married, she would give up her survivor benefits and receive a Social Security check that constituted only half of my father's.

You could call this the marriage penalty—on Geritol. I like to tease my father and say that the government is actually encouraging sin among the aged. The reality is that for many people, like my father and his girlfriend, Social Security is the only system for paying for retirement. As a result, my father's lifestyle choices are circumscribed by the Social Security rules. This is not an outcome that anyone would wish to see continue. Social Security is, indeed, a mess, and the way it has been mismanaged over the decades is an abiding shame.

Make No Mistake …

It's important to make the best possible decision about when to elect for Social Security benefits, so that we can have the best shot at receiving what should have been ours all along.

4

Mistake #8: Picking the Wrong Investments

When I first started to outline this book, I intended to call this chapter "Improper Portfolio Construction," but somehow that didn't seem sexy enough. Portfolio construction? That sounds like something that only affects a true Daddy Warbucks. Your "average" millionaire—the individual worth, say, less than $5 million—may not even be conscious of the fact that all of his or her assets actually add up to a portfolio, or that any construction is required.

But if you've got those kinds of numbers, it's all too easy to construct a portfolio in a fashion that doesn't maximize your returns. That's a very fancy and polite way of saying that it's very easy to make bad investment decisions, for a lot of reasons. In this chapter, I'd like to explore with you the eight most common errors to which even wealthy individuals and couples fall prey.

Expecting Steady Returns

Ever heard anything like this before? "I've got a million bucks invested. So if I can get 8 percent plus Social Security, I'm good!"

Not so fast, my friend! The problem is that the market fluctuates. Even if the market is up 6, 8, or 15 percent over an extended period of time, you never know what's going to happen in any given year. A recent study showed that the S&P went up on average 11.1 percent, but in two-thirds of those years, the return was either above 21 percent or below 1 percent. In other words, imagine a trading band around that 11.1 percent figure. That band stretches 10 percent to the plus side and 10 percent to the minus side. So we're talking about a range from a gain of 1.1 percent in a year all the way up to a gain of 21.1 percent. Remarkably, two out of every three years that study measured found that the S&P gained—or lost—outside of that range.

What does that mean to you? It means that there's no such thing as being able to count on any percent gain from your investments. This matters because money grows very differently if it bounces around like that, without a steady percentage rate attached to it. And the market doesn't just fluctuate positively—it fluctuates negatively as well. This means that our portfolios will have down years mixed in with the up years.

Why does this matter?

1. Losses count more than gains.

Volatility is terrifying. Since market returns fluctuate, it's important to keep in mind that losses count more than gains.

Let's examine the situations of three imaginary investors, Alice, Bob, and Carl. We'll start with Alice.

She had a bad year, sorry to say, and her portfolio has gone down by 10 percent over the course of a year. This means that she has 90 percent of her portfolio left. What does she need to be back where she was at the beginning of the first year?

If you guessed 10 percent, you're close.

But it's not 10 percent—it's 11 percent. When your portfolio loses money, you need an even larger gain to wipe out that loss.

Bob did even worse, if that's any consolation to Alice. His portfolio was down by 25 percent, so all he has at the end of the year is 75 percent of his original portfolio. What does Bob need, aside from a new stockbroker? He needs the market to go up 33 percent to win back the 25 percent he lost. It's tough to be Bob right now.

But it's even worse to be Carl. Carl's portfolio dropped by 50 percent, bringing to mind Woody Allen's observation that "a stockbroker is someone who invests your money until there's nothing left." Carl's doing the math in his head, and he realizes that he needs his portfolio to *double* in order to get back to even keel. So we see that losses truly count for more than gains.

Why does this matter to you? Once you enter retirement, you are a net seller of shares and a net redeemer of investments for the rest of your life. So you need a completely different way to manage money in your retirement. You might think that the example of Carl, who lost 50 percent of his portfolio, is extreme, or something I threw in just to illustrate a point. Unfortunately, that number is torn from the headlines.

Remember the bear market we had in the early 2000s? (I'm sure you're trying to forget it.) S&P dropped 50 percent in just a couple of years. Unfortunately, the world is full of individuals who thought that the tech boom was going to fund their entire retirement. Instead, the tech collapse simply postponed their retirement. Ouch.

When you're working, you can invest for growth. If the market bounces around, there's no problem. You've got time on your side. When you are retired, however, you need both growth and income. This calls for special techniques for portfolio management. Unfortunately, most individual investors do not know how to shift their portfolio from growth to a model that allows for *both* growth and income. What's worse, even many investment professionals don't know how to make that shift.

When you retire, there's no need to go to a horror movie for entertainment. Just turn on CNBC and you'll get all the fears you can handle, or maybe more. Volatility is terrifying to retirees. Those out of their working years sweat bullets even in a market that's treading water, let alone one in decline. It's vital, therefore, to counteract the volatility and variability of the market so as to preserve your portfolio and yet still provide for income and growth. You need sophisticated software programs that allow variability to be figured into the mix. These programs project a range of results with a high degree of confidence. Also, when you properly diversify, you smooth out the annual return on your investment. This gets you off that nasty volatility merry-go-round.

So the mistaken belief is that in order to achieve portfolio growth, people need years in which the market goes up 20 percent. The reality is that if you can avoid the big losses, you'll be just fine—as long as you and your investment advisor understand that volatility must be accounted for in your portfolio management system.

2. Using a Short-Term Investment Horizon

The second bad investment decision people make is to truncate or shorten their investment horizon. New clients often tell me, "Steve, I'm retiring in five years, so I need a conservative program for my money." That's simply not true! I have to remind my clients that they're going to *retire* in five years, not die. Your actual investment horizon is your entire lifetime. Just because you retire doesn't mean your money has to quit working, too. Make sure that you are not using a short-term investment horizon. The date of your retirement is not the date on which your investment planning ceases.

3. Paying Too Much Attention to the Media

Thirty years ago, if you wanted to watch financial news on TV, you had one choice: Wait for Friday night's *Wall $treet Week* with Louis Rukeyser. If you didn't like what you heard from Rukeyser, pretty much your only alternative was *Sanford and Son*, and you sure didn't hear a lot of great investment advice from Redd Foxx.

Thanks to all the new media, times have changed. There are myriad sources of "news" competing—even jostling and shouting—for our attention. You don't have just one or two thirty-minute shows each week—you've got investment "guidance" 24/7/365. And we watch, and we watch, and we watch.

Like many people, I watch CNBC in the morning, while I'm working out in my home gym. They'll typically have some analyst tell us what stocks to watch that day. But have we truly become a nation of day traders? The typical investor—certainly the investor in his or her fifties, sixties, and beyond—is not likely to get in or out of any given stock on any given day. Yet, we all seem focused on this incredibly narrow, short-term goal.

The only thing they ought to be telling us on these financial news programs is this: Figure your risk tolerance, put together appropriate asset allocation, watch your fund managers, and don't fiddle with your investments. That's it! That's really all you need to know about investing. It's so simple and obvious, but this vital truth becomes obfuscated in the noisy battle for financial news ratings. This is why you'll probably never see me on CNBC—because as soon as I see that red light go on, I'll look into the camera, smile, and say, "Figure your risk tolerance, figure your asset allocation, watch your fund managers, and don't fiddle. Pick an advisor to help you with this so you avoid making emotion-based decisions about your money. Let your advisor take care of the details and choose the right managers, and then go play golf."

The simplest advice is the soundest advice. Ignore the shouting on TV. Their whole approach—to focus you on the short, short, short term, in order to pretend to have "news" to talk about—is a lot like driving a car but staring only one foot ahead of where your front bumper is. You could drive off a cliff and not know it until it was too late. Same with investing the "new media" way.

By the way, the biggest mistake people make when choosing fund managers is to concentrate too closely on the immediate past track records of the managers. For example, some people choose managers whose previous year was very successful. And others, even very sophisticated investors, eschew those managers who had two bad quarters. The reality is that even top fund managers aren't successful every single quarter. Just because someone has a great year doesn't mean he's about to have another one. And just because he had a couple of bad quarters doesn't mean he's never going to have a great six months right away. So choosing the right group of managers (in each area of differentiation: large cap, medium cap, small cap, international, etc.) is a little more complicated than just looking at the managers' immediate past results.

4. Attempting Market Timing and Chasing Returns

What did your grandfather tell you about investing in the stock market? Buy low, sell high? So why do so few people do just that?

If you knew which way the market was going, investing would be easy. The problem is that you never know ahead of time whether it's headed up or down. As a result, people tend to chase returns. If the market is going up, they feel good and so put their money in. The converse holds true as well: If the market is going down, everybody gets nervous and pulls out their money. People want to get out before the "other guy" does.

The only problem is that the "other guy" is Warren Buffett, and he's buying while you sell and selling while you buy. By the time the crowd gets to the Buffett table, the pickings are pretty slim. This is true in the stock market, it's true in real estate, and it's true in any venue of investment where pros and regular folks jostle on an unequal playing field.

If you got caught up in the tech boom, you're not alone. One person who didn't buy into the idea that the business cycle had been repealed and that it was perfectly okay to buy businesses for 250 times next year's earnings was that same Warren Buffett. If you remember the late nineties, everybody looked at Buffett and said, "The old man's lost it! Value investing is dead—as is the business cycle!"

Buffett even apologized to his investors. "I don't understand tech stocks," he said. "I don't understand why Bill Gates's stock is going for 200 times next year's earnings." Well, we all know what happened next. The NASDAQ dropped from 5,000 all the way down to 1,200, which meant that all those people who were telling you how the game had passed Buffett by now needed to find an investment that would give them a return of 300+ percent—just so that they could get back to even. It was a bloodbath, and the people who got hurt the most were the ones who jumped in when the wave had already headed toward the top—then crashed.

Let's take a look at a broader range of time—the years from 1984 to 2000. This was a huge, upward-moving market that lasted sixteen years. Dalbar Inc. and Lipper Inc. made a study of those years that indicated that a monkey throwing darts at a financial page pinned to the wall of their cages could have made real money. How much money? The average stock fund had a 14 percent annual return during that period. So, how did the individual investors do, those who moved in and out of those stock funds?

They only made 5.3 percent.

Where did their money go? It's easy to blame loads, fees, and commissions. But the reality is that people made only 5.3 percent on their money when they could have had a 14 percent annual return because they were chasing returns and attempting to time the market. It just never works.

The reality of investor psychology is that if the market is going down, we think it's going to go down even further, so we sell. If it's going up, surely that means that the water is safe, and it's only going to go up more, and so we throw more money in. Not many people put money in when the market is low. Typically, when the stock market is bottoming, mutual fund redemptions soar.

This is insane. We baby boomers should be pumping money into the stock market, especially when it's low. We should be net buyers, but we're not. We're market timers. We chase returns. And we blow it ... time after time after time.

A Franklin Templeton study confirms what most of us suspect: If you miss the best ten or twenty trading days of the year, you miss all the gains. This study analyzed a four-year period comprising 1,263 trading days. If you missed the best forty days of that period—the best ten days each year—you would have been better off in a treasury bill than going in and out of the market. Yet none of us thinks this way.

We make our gains in a relatively short period of time. The market might scream for a month or so, creating the entire return for the year. But if we hang out on the sidelines and miss those key days, we miss out on all the gains. And the same thing is true on the down side. It doesn't "feel good" to buy things when they're low. We assume that things are worth whatever price is set on them, so if assets are inexpensive, they must not be any good.

Buying low, which is the first half of the famous "Buy low, sell high" equation, feels like eating broccoli. We just don't want to do it. Ironically, broccoli is perhaps the most nutritious, perfect food on the planet. But you don't see too many people rolling into McDonald's and asking to get their broccoli super-sized. As I quoted Warren Buffett at the beginning of this book, "Human nature is always in conflict with successful investing."

This is just as true for the amateur as it is for the top professional. I remember back in early 2002, one of my clients suggested that she get out of the stock market. It turned out she was right. The Iraq War was about to begin, and the market tumbled due to insecurity about oil and other factors. I called my client every other week and asked her the same question: "When are we going back into the market?" Getting out is only a good call if you have the discipline to go back in when the market's down. Now, instead of applying a good disciplined strategy, she's trying to read her crystal ball.

My client didn't feel good about going back into the market until the market had already bounced back. In other words, by pulling her money out and not getting it back into the market in time, she lost out. If you're going to perform market timing, you've got to get *both* the "in" and the "out" right—you can't just hit one of them.

Professionals suffer from the same problem. Take the case of Abby Joseph Cohen, for years one of the most respected analysts on Wall Street. People religiously followed her market guidance, which led to her becoming a managing director at Goldman Sachs and getting ranked by *Forbes* as one of The World's Most Powerful Women. Only one problem. She made one misstep in the market, one time when she advised people to make a move—and that single misstep wiped out *the entire value* of all of her great calls.

The point is that if you're trying to time the market and chase returns, you're not alone. The problem is that everybody else loses money that way, too.

5. Honey, I Shrunk the Portfolio!

The easiest way to shrink your portfolio is to do asset allocation once and never rebalance it. Here's what happens. You do your homework. You create an asset allocation model that makes the most sense, given your tolerance for risk and loss and the nature of the investments you think are the wisest for you. And then you'll let it go. What happens?

Your successful choices will represent a bulge in your portfolio. They will represent a much higher percentage of your portfolio than you had initially intended. What goes up, comes down ... so take some of your winnings off the table and rebalance, but just enough to get back to your original allocation.

Think back to the tech boom and subsequent bust. The investors who were hardest hit were those who failed to rebalance their portfolios. Instead of taking some of the tech money off the table, they let the money ride. As a result, they ended up losing their gains ... and then some.

6. Not Adjusting Your Risk Posture As You Approach Retirement

Retirement shouldn't come as a surprise. How many of us actually find ourselves saying, "My goodness! I'm suddenly sixty-four years and eleven months old, and I'm going to retire in a month. I should have thought of that sooner."

We generally know years in advance when our expected retirement date will be. The wise investor adjusts his or her risk posture as retirement approaches. We want to move slowly in the direction of moderation for the first years prior to our retirement. It's tough, from either a financial or psychological perspective, to adjust to a moderate portfolio overnight.

The best time to get conservative is after the market has gone up. That's when you want to take some of your gains off the table, trim your stocks, and go to fixed-income investments and cash. And yet, if you're like most people, your gut won't let you do it. When you've been investing for growth for so long, it's psychologically very difficult to make a move to bonds and cash. It just feels like something old people do. The last thing baby boomers want is to think of themselves as old.

Give yourself time to moderate the nature of your portfolio to reflect your changing needs. Redirecting a portfolio is a lot like turning an aircraft carrier. It takes some time to make the turn. Give yourself the time you need.

7. Failing To Coordinate the Entire Portfolio

Chances are, your money is in many different places. You might have a 401(k) at an old job, money in various bank accounts here and where you used to live, in your wife's account, in the sock drawer, and maybe in a coffee can buried in your front lawn. Many investors fail to consider the big picture when it comes to their money. You've got to look at all your money in order to make all of it work the hardest for you.

What's the penalty? You might not have the diversification you thought you had if you cannot see all of your assets at one time. You can also save money on taxes, depending on where you do the rebalancing. If you can see all of your assets in a single glance—on a piece of paper or computer screen—you'll be in a much stronger position when it comes to making decisions. You can save considerable money on taxes depending on where in your portfolio you perform the rebalancing that may be necessary. First look to your retirement assets, because you can delay taxes even further with money in qualified accounts.

The main thing: Keep your eye on the big picture.

8. Not Titling Your Accounts To Coordinate with Your Estate Planning

That sounds like a lot of jargon. Here's a way to understand this concept. What if I offered you a $2,000 investment that would give you a return of $1,000,000—and it's all legal? Let me show you how it works.

In most states, what you hold jointly with your spouse goes to the survivor when you die. Let's say you're worth $4 million. When you pass away, your spouse gets that whole sum. But when they die, estate taxes will amount to one quarter of that.

What if you had separated those assets while you were still alive and kept $2 million in each name? Your estate tax would be zero.

In this scenario, retitling your accounts and setting up the right trusts will cost you around $2,000 and save you a million dollars in estate tax. It's not going to affect you, and it won't even affect your spouse. It will certainly have a negative effect on your kids, who rightly could have asked, "Where's that extra million?"

Correct answer: Washington.

What the government really ought to do in cases like this is to send a thank you note to your kids that says something like this: "We used your money to carry on the Iraq War for one day and still had enough left over to make 500 Social Security payments to people you've never met. Thanks for the money!"

It takes a very short amount of time to create the trusts and to title your accounts to coordinate with your estate planning. The peace of mind you'll receive, not to mention the bequests coming the way of your children and grandchildren, will be well worth the time and money.

◆   ◆   ◆

What's the thread that runs through all of these points? The fact that we are making emotional decisions instead of rational ones. We are so emotionally tied to our money that it is hard to think rationally about it. It's easy for someone else to be disciplined with your money, which is why people turn to people like me. Managing our own money is hard, because we make so many of our important buying decisions based on emotion rather than logic.

If you want an example, think about the last time you stepped onto the lot of a car dealership. The slick car salesman hustled over to you and said things like, "Imagine yourself feeling that rich Corinthian leather! Imagine that 4.5-valve, 600-horsepower engine responding to the touch of your foot!" I'm not a car guy, as you might have just guessed, but those sorts of statements do turn many of us on. We do get excited about the idea of having a red car versus a white one, a German car instead of a Japanese model. These are emotional decisions, my friend, not logical ones—and I'll swear to that on a stack of *Car and Driver* magazines.

Make No Mistake …

If you're going to spend a few extra thousand dollars to get yourself a car that's going to make your heart race, fine. You've earned the right to do so. But when it comes to your investment future, it's time to get the emotion out so that you can start making the best possible decisions for yourself, your spouse, and your children and grandchildren.

5

Mistake #7: Not Paying Attention to Your Life Insurance and Annuity Policies

Bye-Bye, Life Insurance!

The overriding mistake people make with life insurance is to keep it when it's no longer necessary. At some point, you will have outgrown your life insurance. You originally bought it so that if you died prematurely and there were not enough assets to cover your financial goals, the insurance would take care of it. Your life insurance would pay off your house, provide education money for the kids, and provide a monthly income support for your spouse now that you are no longer in the picture.

But take a look around. Your kids have graduated college (although they may well be living in your basement). You've paid off the house. There's more than enough in the bank to take care of your spouse's financial needs for the rest of his or her life, whether you're there or not. You don't need life insurance for the purpose of covering things if you die prematurely. So what do you do with your policies?

If it's term life, drop it immediately. At this point, it's a bad investment for you (if it was ever a good investment in the first place).

If it's whole life or some other life insurance product with cash value, then we've got something to talk about. Let's say you've been paying $6,000 a year for twenty years and the policy now has a cash value of $80,000. If you sold the policy at a loss, that $40,000 loss wouldn't be deductible. Of course, if you sold it for a gain, you would pay tax on the gain. (Just another reason why we don't like our tax laws.) So how can you deduct that loss?

The answer is to perform a tax-free exchange from your life insurance policy to an annuity policy. Your cost basis comes over. As a result, you won't have to pay tax on that $40,000 gain if the annuity value grows back to $120,000. If you need cash, do the exchange in year one and take the loss in year two in order to pull out the money and preserve the loss for tax purposes. (If you didn't know you could do a tax-free exchange from life insurance into an annuity, don't feel bad. Even most accountants and financial planners and other wealth advisors don't know about it. But that's why you're reading this book!)

Don't Forget the Annuities

Most people I know who have purchased annuities tend to do the same thing with them: put them in a file and forget all about 'em.

Sound familiar?

If so, you're not alone. After all, we're talking about the ten most *common* mistakes that people make with their money, not the ten most bizarre ones. I'm just trying to share with you what I see every day. So if this scenario applies to you, don't feel bad. Instead, I hope you'll use the information in this chapter to maximize the value of your annuities and your life insurance.

Turn Those Annuities Into Cash Flow

Let's say you put $100,000 into an annuity some years ago, and now it's worth $250,000. Your spouse is excited—and so is Uncle Sam. If you decided that you wanted to take out $50,000 a year, I've got bad news: The entire $50,000 is taxable, even though only 60 percent of the money that you're taking out is a capital gain by any rational measure.

I know—it's a weird way to tax assets. It's also the method of taxation that's most beneficial to the government. Are you surprised? I thought not. The way the government sees it, the first money you take out from your annuity is taxable. Your investment, in their mind, comes out last. In short, they found a way to accelerate the tax that you pay on the gain on your deferred annuity.

So what do you do about it? Annuitize the annuity. Go to your insurance company and ask for an income stream. That way, the IRS says that some of the money that comes out is taxable, and some is your own money coming back. In IRS terms, you get to "claim a ratable return of your cost basis." For lay people, that simply means that you don't have to pay tax on everything you get. On an after-tax basis, therefore, you end up getting to keep more money if you annuitize your annuity than if you don't.

You Better Shop Around

The old Motown song was right. When it comes to annuities, it's important to keep your insurance company honest. Ask them how much of an income stream they'll offer you based on your annuity. Then shop your annuity with other insurance companies. Make sure it's an apples to apples comparison. You, or your investment advisor, should say, "If you had an individual with this date of birth, with this amount of money in the annuity, and seeking a six-year payout, how much would you give?"

Remarkably, you can do a tax-free exchange on annuities similar to the tax-free exchange on real estate with which many investors are familiar. The important thing to consider (if you're planning on such an exchange) is the financial strength of the insurance companies. Deal only with financially sound carriers. A fly-by-night might offer you a better rate, but, to keep our sixties music theme alive, will they still love you—and pay you—tomorrow?

Psst! Wanna Buy a Slightly Used Life Insurance Policy?

If your life insurance has cash value, you may be able to sell the policy and get some cash right now. Entities called life insurance settlement companies exist. This came about at the beginning of the AIDS epidemic in the early 1980s, when there were plenty of individuals who had little or no money for health care, but plenty of money coming to their survivors and beneficiaries after they passed away. As a result, a resale market for life insurance policies came into existence. This process allowed AIDS sufferers to sell their policies and get cash to pay for their healthcare needs.

Life insurance settlement companies now work with just about any individual who owns an insurance policy with cash value. These companies will look at your policy and make you an offer based on your age and your health.

A client of mine divorced her husband and received his insurance policy in the divorce. Her husband was quite ill and she was making high premium payments in order to keep the policy current. The policy had a cash value of $40,000, and she was able to sell it for $60,000. This way, she did not have to continue to make payments until her former husband passed away.

This resale market for life insurance policies typically begins for individuals who are sixty or older and offers a very nice way to get out of a life insurance policy you no longer need.

Along the same lines, don't make the mistake of planning to run out of money at the average mortality, which for older people in today's society is around eighty-five. Remember that "average" means half of us will outlive that eighty-five-year mark. There was a book not too many years ago that urged its readers to "die broke" and that the last check they write should cover their funeral costs. But what if you last one day longer than you expected? What are you going to eat that day? Where are you going to live? Don't plan your portfolio to run out at any age. You just might go further than your money!

Don't Mention the Pension

Companies that offer pensions are fewer and farther between than ever, but they still exist. The issue we want to consider here is whether to opt for a 50 percent interest in your pension for your survivor should you die first. Under ERISA, you are entitled to take that option. Most people take it automatically, but they fail to realize that it reduces their benefit while they're still alive. Let's look at the numbers.

Let's say that you would receive $3,000 a month under your pension. If you take the 50 percent survivor benefit, you would only get $2,500 a month now, and your surviving spouse would only get $1,250 a month after you pass. In short, that 50 percent interest in your pension is like life insurance, because you're giving up something today for something that happens when you die. If you're healthy and insurable, get your own life insurance policy for the same amount or less money, in order to get a survivor benefit. If your spouse predeceases you, you can't go back and undo your choice. You'll be stuck at that lower level for the rest of your life. Of course, if you remarry, your new spouse would get the survivor benefit if you pass first. Who says you can't buy true love?

Insurance Equals Flexibility

If you die, she becomes a survivor, so she gets the insurance benefits. If she dies first and you survive, take out the cash value of the policy and stop paying premiums. If you both live a long time, cash in the life insurance policy at eighty-five and do something fun with it. Take your family on a nice vacation. Buy a time share. Go to Vegas and bet it all on the roulette wheel. You've already won at the game of life, so you've got the hot dice!

On the other hand, if you go down the survivor benefit route instead of the insurance route, the money would be gone if you both lived. In short, the survivor benefit is the equivalent of a zero cash value, non-cancelable life insurance policy. If that doesn't sound too appealing to you, well, I feel the same way. Do your own math and see if it makes sense.

Who Owns the Policy?

Let's say you bought whole life insurance or some other insurance with a cash value some years ago. Now you've got assets, so you no longer need insurance to replace an income stream if you die. Instead, you want your insurance to pay any estate tax when you pass. What do you do?

Back then, when you bought the policy, the beneficiary didn't matter, because it came within estate tax limits. My suggestion: Change the ownership. Have someone other than yourself own the policy so that it doesn't pass into your estate. If you give the policy to your grown children or put it into a trust, you can get it out of your estate. There are certain caveats. You've got to live three years after you make this change, and there are some other potholes that your insurance advisor can point out to you. But you definitely want to make sure that your life insurance does not end up in your taxable estate when you die.

Make No Mistake …

When you retire, it's a great time to review all of your annuity and life insurance policies. Your objectives, risk tolerance, and cash needs have all changed. Make sure that your policies represent the way your financial life actually looks today. You'll be glad you did, and so will those who rely on you.

6

Mistake #6: Having an Anemic 401(k)

You very likely have a 401(k) plan through your employer. It might surprise you to learn that your employer isn't too thrilled about having to offer 401(k) plans. They're expensive to maintain, complicated for employees to deal with and a compliance and accounting headache. Yet, if employers wish to remain competitive in the job marketplace, they've got to provide them.

Your employer, like all employers, is in the business of making money by offering products, services, or both. Any time devoted to employee issues, like 401(k) plans or pensions, is on the "no pay" side of the ledger. Your retirement plan is a benefit to you, but it's a real cost to your employer in terms of money, time, and resources. As a result, many employers don't spend the time it takes to provide their employees with the best possible range of investment options.

So the million-dollar mistake we're going to investigate in this chapter is how to be proactive when it comes to evaluating your employer's retirement offerings, how to get the most out of them, and knowing when to take your money out and move it somewhere else.

The advice I want to share with you in this chapter boils down to four points:

1. Fully fund your plan.

2. Pay attention to it.

3. Get out when you retire.

4.   If you have a pension, make the right choice when it comes to tak-
     ing a lump sum or getting a payout.

Max It Out!

There's no reason *not* to contribute the maximum to your 401(k) plan.
Not everyone makes the maximum contribution, simply because they cannot afford to do so. If you're reading this book, you're most likely in a
position where you can afford to spare the cash in order to maximize your
plan. The beautiful thing about a 401(k) plan is that you pay no income
tax on the money you invest and it grows in a tax-deferred environment.
This allows you to maximize your investment accumulation. What's more,
most companies offer a matching program, up to a certain percentage. For
example, some will match 50 percent of what you contribute up to 6 percent of pay, which means you're actually getting an extra 3 percent just for
investing in your own future.

I've heard all the arguments against fully funding a 401(k) plan. The
basic argument is that if you invest outside a 401(k) or an IRA, then you're
subject to a lower capital gains tax when you liquidate the asset. But you
take such a big tax hit up front that it's hard—almost impossible—to find
the kind of investments that will do for you what your 401(k) plan can.

How much are we talking about? In 2006, the IRS allowed you to defer
$15,000 worth of income by placing it in a 401(k). It gets better: If you're
over fifty, you can put in an additional $5,000 tax-free. The government
calls this a "catch-up" additional contribution, and it's one of the best
things about turning fifty. It sure is a lot better than your qualification for
membership in the AARP!

Let's do the math. If you put $20,000 in your retirement plan, how
much money do you have to invest? That's right—$20,000! On the other
hand, if you kept that $20,000 out of the 401(k), you'll have to pay tax on
it right now. If you're affluent, you can expect to pay 40 percent. In other
words, $8,000 goes right to the government, which means you're already
behind what your investment would be worth if it were sitting in the
401(k). Can you invest the remaining $12,000 to grow on an after-tax

basis to catch up to the $20,000 you put in your 401(k)? If you can, give me a call. I'd like to get in on that investment, too!

The smartest thing you can do right now is maximize your contribution to your 401(k). The only individuals to whom this does not apply are those who expect to be in a higher tax bracket upon retirement than during their working years. Certainly there are such individuals out there, but they are the exception to the rule.

Open Those Envelopes!

Mind your money. It seems like such obvious advice, but it's remarkable how many affluent people fail to heed it. Typically, the individual receives a quarterly statement from the financial service company managing the 401(k) plan and just takes a quick look at the bottom-line figure. As long as it has steadily increased, that's all they want to know. This is true because many individuals fear that they lack the expertise to properly allocate money among different investment options. So the path of least resistance is to "file and forget"—to glance at the number, stick the envelope in a drawer, and forget about the whole thing.

Unfortunately, the typical investor, operating without any sort of guidance, does a fairly poor job of investing his or her money. The fear of loss is indeed greater than the desire for gain, so people do all kinds of things in order to avoid losses. The problem is that the actions they take end up losing them more money than if they had done nothing at all. That kind of negative feedback creates a situation where people are afraid to take any action, right or wrong, for fear that they will only make things worse. What should you be doing? What is an intelligent approach to managing one's own 401(k) plan?

The wise course is to study the investment alternatives (typically, mutual funds) that your 401(k) plan offers. Identify the ones that have the best track records, the ones that are the best funds in their category. Don't think that you've got to use every single investment choice that your employer has made available to you. Chances are that there might be just a few really good options, and the rest are mediocre or even poor investments. Continue to monitor the investments compared to others in the same category (large cap domestic stock, international stock, etc.) and don't dump them for just one sub-par yearly result. Our research indicates the very best mutual funds over the long haul only exceeded their relevant benchmark in two out of three years. So you want to give these managers a chance to show their stuff. Nobody holds the most rewarding stocks every single year.

If your employer loves you so much, why isn't he offering you only world-class mutual funds? The simple fact is that most employers don't spend a lot of time touching up their list of investment options. They'll spend time on the front end, doing due diligence in order to find the right provider. But once they've got a plan in place, they really don't want to monkey with it. Changes to the 401(k) plan trigger confusion and often fear on the part of the participants. Employers simply don't want to incur the cost of educating their plan participants about new options. You could call it Morton's First Law of Investing: Investments at rest tend to remain at rest. Inertia is the driving force, not your financial best interests.

401(k) Plans Make You Money … but Not Your Employer

Even the big national providers offer a lot of mediocre choices for 401(k) plans. They won't come right out and admit they have some stinkers, but that doesn't mean it isn't so. It's up to you to sort through the options in your plan and identify and stick with the winners.

It gets worse. Some employers are afraid of incurring liability if they make too many changes in their plans, and some even avoid riskier areas altogether, like small-cap stock funds. And some employers just throw up their hands altogether and say, "We don't know what we're doing, so we'll go to Vanguard and get some index funds." Index funds can be great investments, but only if you know how to mix and match the index funds into a well-orchestrated portfolio. Most employees don't know how to do this. As a result, you may not be getting the best results.

There really is a battle of needs going on. You need a way to maximize your retirement savings, while the employer needs to reduce costs with regard to liability, employee education, disrupting workflow, and similar matters. Your financial future is not their priority, and maintaining the optimal 401(k) plan is not in their best financial interest.

When we manage a 401(k), we keep track of fund managers who leave a fund and go elsewhere. We want to know why they left, who's taking over, and what those good managers are going to do next. Employers typically don't even replace the fund. They just leave it there, and their attitude is, well, good luck to you. That's just not good enough, but it is reality, so do your homework!

Keep the Big Picture in Mind

Not all of your different investments have to reflect your overall allocation strategy. In other words, you want to have a nice mix of stock and fixed-income investments, depending on your age and risk tolerance. You don't have to have a situation in which every single one of your investment accounts reflects the overall mix of your investment strategy.

That's why it's so important to look at the big picture. Your 401(k) plan may offer one or two great investment opportunities ... and five dogs. It's tough to construct a balanced portfolio from that sort of combination. So put all your 401(k) money into the few investments that are real winners and ignore the stinkers. Then structure the rest of your portfolio (IRA and personal accounts) around those investments in your 401(k) so that you achieve balance across all of your investments combined.

Remember: You don't have to have each separate portfolio reflecting your overall strategy. You can have your large-cap fund in your 401(k), your international fund in your IRA, your bonds somewhere else, etc. What matters is that the big picture reflects your overall approach to investing. If you only have a couple good options in your 401(k), select those options and then construct the rest of your portfolio around those investment vehicles.

Know When To Fold 'Em

When you retire, don't make the million-dollar mistake of leaving your 401(k) plan at your employer, who has only a limited number of investment options. You can buy ten thousand different investment products through Schwab or other discount brokers. Can your employer come close? Not likely. You can find a much more robust lineup of investment choices by taking your money out of your 401(k) when you retire and moving it elsewhere. This way, you won't be stuck with the plan's idea of what a good investment strategy should look like. You'll have the freedom to invest that money as you see fit, free from the limitations that your employer's plan imposes.

The key point here is to orchestrate your rollover properly, from the trustee of your 401(k) plan to the custodian of the IRA. Here's the critical factor: Don't take your 401(k) money as a distribution. If you do, your employer will automatically withhold 20 percent as tax. A lot of people don't realize how much money they even have until they get their 401(k) distribution check. They're assuming that the nice number they see on that check is 100 percent of the money in their plan, and then they roll it over into an IRA, never realizing that that plan was 20 percent short of what it could have been. And if these individuals are younger than age fifty-nine and a half taking some form of early retirement, they are subject to an additional 10 percent penalty for early withdrawal on top of taxation on the 20% withheld. This frequently results in a total tax hit of half of what didn't make it to your IRA!

Don't let this happen to you. Roll over your 401(k) plan into an IRA *without* taking it as a distribution.

Here's another reason for doing so. If you die and your money is still in your 401(k) plan at work, there's no way to allow your heirs to take it out over their life expectancies. As we saw in an earlier chapter, $100,000 that you stick in an IRA and leave to a grandchild could be worth seven figures over the course of his or her lifetime. That won't happen if your money is still stuck in your 401(k) plan at the time of your death.

In that case, your beneficiaries will typically have just five years to withdraw all the money. Honestly, this is only fair to employers. Why should they pay administration fees for the management of your money during the entire lifetime of your children? The technique you want to investigate is the "stretch IRA," which leaves your money first to your wife and then to your children. With a stretch IRA, your children can withdraw that money over their entire life expectancy.

I'm hard-pressed to think of a single reason for leaving your money in your employer's 401(k) after you can get your money out. The IRA into which you can roll over that money is just as creditor-proof as your 401(k), and the tax benefits are the same. There are certain rare circumstances where it does make sense to leave the money, but these relate only to individuals over seventy who are working for companies in which they do not possess a 5 percent interest. If that's not you, take the money and run.

A Lump in Your Throat ... and Your Wallet

As we have discussed earlier, the traditional pension plan is not nearly as popular today, due to employer cost and risk. They are getting to become as rare as the proverbial gold watch. Nevertheless, many companies still offer pensions, and yours might be one of them. So what's the most efficient way for you to maximize the money that's coming to you?

In an earlier chapter, we discussed the spousal survival feature and the election you must make as to whether you want your spouse to receive benefits after you die. In this chapter, I'd like to take a look at a different issue, that of lump-sum distribution versus a lifetime income stream.

The key question is this: Just how well funded is your company's plan? Yes, it's enticing to get a lifetime income stream, but what if you worked for Enron or WorldCom? Those checks are awfully hard to cash these days. Psychologically, everybody loves the idea that "My company will keep paying me even though I'm not going into work!" And there is a certain amount of psychic comfort in getting a check from the same company that has paid you all these years. But if you've got pension money, the question is this: Should you take it all right now and forego those psychic benefits? Or should you let it ride and enjoy that income stream?

With more and more companies defaulting on their pensions, you've got to ask what kind of return you could make on the money if you managed it yourself. I understand that it's frightening for many retirees to invest money themselves and create their own income stream. A lot of my clients tell me, "At this point in my life, I don't want to be responsible for these issues anymore." I understand that. Yet there are a couple great ways to develop income streams by using financial service firms. Investment management firms and insurance companies are two great alternatives. You could buy a variable annuity in order to create an income stream if you take the lump sum right now.

Modern day annuity contracts have attractive guarantees against loss and provide income streams for life. Many of these contracts have the capability to produce increasing income streams over time. The problem is that you've got to decide who is more likely to survive—you, or your employer and what alternatives are appropriate for you to consider.

Make No Mistake ...

The major mistake that employees make is failing to maximize their 401(k) plan investments and then failing to keep an eye on those investments. At the same time, we can stay too long at the fair by failing to remove our 401(k) money once we retire. And if you are fortunate enough to have an employer offering you a pension, consider all the factors before you elect the lump sum or the income stream.

Will your employer still be there in ten or fifteen years? Is the income stream competitive with alternative and more personalized investment approaches? Are you willing to forego the psychic benefits of letting your employer handle your money and create an income stream for you? Examine all the possible solutions, and I know you'll come to the right answer.

7

Mistake #5: Staying Put

You chose your neighborhood thirty years ago perhaps because it had really good schools or offered a fairly easy commute to work. But the kids have been out of the house for years (except for your youngest, who came home after college and has been living comfortably in your basement). You've retired, or are about to, or you're working for a company at some distance from where you currently live. You and your spouse have taken up golf, but there are not a lot of golf courses nearby, or the climate may simply be inhospitable to golf for six or seven months of the year. And yet, if you're like many people in their late fifties and up, you do nothing about it.

The purpose of this chapter is to suggest that you get moving! Most affluent individuals sixty and older will move at least once during their retirement years. The simple fact is that where you live may no longer meet your needs. You may have far too much house than you really want. You may have shut down rooms or an entire wing so that you don't have to maintain it. Or perhaps there's too much backyard to care for, or not enough space for that rose or vegetable garden you've always wanted.

It's not a fatal mistake to stay put, but now that you can afford to do whatever you want, wouldn't it be nice to live in a place—or in two places—where all those dreams and activities can take place?

I'd like to share with you an exercise called the ideal week. You take three days, and your spouse takes three days. What would be perfect for you to do in those three days? What leisure time activities do you enjoy? What kinds of places do you like to visit? The golf course, the museum, the beach? Think about more than one season when you make this determination. I'm writing this in the summer, so boating, fishing, and hiking come readily to mind. But an ideal winter day for me involves skiing, skiing, and more skiing. So it may well be that in order to enjoy your ideal day, you'll need more than one home—and there's nothing wrong with that. In fact, as I discussed in Chapter 2, it's possible to save enough money in taxes that you can essentially have that second location ... for free.

Once you've done this exercise, compare your three perfect days with your spouse's three perfect days and then ask yourself, "Is it possible to experience those activities and people right here, where we live now?" For many retirees, the answer is no, simply because their needs and interests have changed. Their friends may have moved south. Their kids may have relocated, perhaps for education or employment. You may have taken up a new hobby or are thinking about starting a new career for which another part of the country would be more suitable. So the thing to do is start thinking about where you'd like to go.

If it's true that many people can have a happier life somewhere other than where they are currently living, why do they stay put? Fear is generally what freezes us in our tracks. There's that subconscious voice that says, "This is the last time I'm going to move!" That only adds to the fear. Give yourself a little slack! Your next move is not necessarily your last move, just as the next car you buy won't necessarily be your last. You may live a lot longer than you realize, especially if you are living a vigorous, active life in which you do the things that you truly enjoy.

In my own case, when I retire, I'll return to Colorado so that I can ski whenever the urge hits me. But when I'm too old to ski—and I hope that day doesn't come for a long time—I wouldn't want to put up with the climate.

Moving implies permanence, and permanence implies the need to get just the right place. Some people can't afford to think about moving. They have to stay where they are for family reasons, so that they can have younger, more able-bodied relatives perform house repairs or such. Chances are, if you're reading this book, you can afford to move, and you should—and you will. I'm here to invite you to open up your mind to what's truly important to you.

One Location Doesn't Fit All

Many of my clients move to Florida. It's nice for much of the year, but it's miserable during June, July, and August. Phoenix, another common retirement destination, can be just as sweltering. On a visit to Phoenix not too long ago, I saw the kickstand of a bicycle literally sinking into the melting blacktop. My feet were burning through the soles of my shoes as I crossed from my car to the store.

That's why having more than one home may be the best idea for you, so that you can take advantage of the good times, and beat the heat—or the cold.

The exercise I suggested a moment ago—thinking about you and your spouse's three ideal days—will help you determine whether where you live now is the most desirable place for your retirement years. In those perfect days, what activities do you see yourself doing? With whom are you spending your time? Who's with you? Why are those things and people important to you—what values dictate your choices? For example, if you envision lots of time with your children and grandchildren, family togetherness is essential for you. If you love the Great Lakes but can't stand the freezing cold, then you are definitely a candidate for multiple homes. The main point is to clarify what matters most to you.

Buy? Or Just Visit?

Many of my clients envision playing with their grandchildren in the sand during summer vacation. That's a beautiful vision, but is it important enough for you to want to live at the beach more than a few weeks a year? While building a house on the Intercoastal Waterway in South Carolina, one of my clients rented a house on the beach. He thought it would be perfect—walk out the door and be jogging on a beach right away. However, it turned out to be the biggest pain he'd ever experienced! Sand, he said, goes everywhere. You can never get all the sand out of your house … or even off your feet. You have to change your sheets daily, or your bed will end up like sandpaper. He couldn't wait to get out of that beach house and into his home on the Intercoastal. So what looks great for a vacation may not work for a full-time residence.

Let me share with you a list of twelve items to consider when you're thinking about where you want to live next. Take a look at each of these twelve items and ask yourself what matters most to you and your spouse.

1. Landscape

2. Climate

3. Quality of life

4. Cost of living

5. Transportation—nearby airport, etc.

6. Retail stores

7. Healthcare services

8. Community services/education

9. Cultural possibilities

10. Recreational activities

11. Work/volunteer activities

12. Crime rates[1]

My wife and I wanted to find a skiing community in Colorado that also offered great educational opportunities. We wanted a place that was a mid-sized city with a growing population so that all the services would be there, but we didn't want anything the size of a Denver, with all the stresses and strains of a big city. So it became fairly easy for us to take out a map and go up and down the Rockies to locate the communities that met with our criteria. The number one choice: the city of Durango.

Our next step was not to buy a house in Durango. Instead, we vacationed there and ultimately fell in love with it. We believe Durango is probably the prettiest part of Colorado, and it offered everything we

---

1.   Check NeighborhoodScout.com or bestplaces.net/crime/or disastercenter.com/crime/

wanted: health care, a good airport, and so on. Our vacation told us that we wanted to explore the community a little further.

We went home and began to read the local Durango newspapers just to get a feel for the rhythm of life. We also did some serious thinking about how close our family—our grandchildren, nieces, and nephews—would be if we lived there. When we realized everything made sense, we bought a condominium and listed it with a management company to rent it out on a short-term basis. That way we're able to stay in our own place when we want to and defray the cost of ownership with rental income when we're not there. That gave us even more important information. We got to see Durango in different seasons, and we also found out in which part of Durango we wanted to live. The other thing we could have done is to rent a place for one to six months to get the same information. In our case, this just didn't fit our family's lifestyle or the kids' school schedule.

Many older people have a resistance toward the idea of renting. They tend to buy instead, because for them, it doesn't feel right to rent. I understand, and yet it can be a good idea to "waste" a few dollars on rent to save yourself the aggravation and potentially bigger dollars if you buy in the wrong place and have to turn around and sell the property that wasn't right for you. First take the vacation, then do the intermediate rental, and then buy, or start building, if that's your choice. The rental makes sense because even if you know that this is the right city for you, how can you know which is the right part of town for you?

When we moved from Colorado to Greensboro, North Carolina, we had no clue about where we wanted to live. So we rented for a year and then figured out exactly what amenities and scenic views we wanted to live near.

The bottom line: Don't commit too soon.

An alternative is to buy rental property—a golf or a ski condo, as we did—and live in it yourself for part of the year. That's a great way to avoid renting and still get the information you need and in the long term you'll even have another income stream.

State of Happiness

If you're going to set up two residences—for example, one in a cooler climate and one in a warmer climate—you want to make sure to claim residency in the state that offers you better tax treatment. If you are retired and withdrawing money from your IRA and generating dividends and interest from your portfolio, you could save $20,000 a year or more—around a quarter of your annual tax bill, depending on the character of your income (capital gains or ordinary income) and the tax rate of the state to which you move. That $20,000 could pay for the upkeep of a home in another state. That's why I say that making the right choice about your state of residency can be extremely important and profitable.

Claiming residency is usually pretty simple. Just be registered to vote in the state in which you wish to claim residency. Get your driver's license there. Register your cars there. Live there six months and a day or more each year. File the Resident's Tax Return in that state. That way you can benefit from the tax advantages that state has to offer.

Your portfolio and retirement income follows the state of your residence, so if you live in a low-tax state, your portfolio income, no matter where the banks or other institutions that hold the money may be located, will be taxed at that low state rate. The only thing that stays behind in your previous state is income that you earned from rental property or business activity in that state. For example, California has a high tax rate. But Nevada is close by and has no state income tax. So you could get a place in Lake Tahoe, on the Nevada side, and claim that as your primary residence. You'll save a ton of state income tax. Of course, if your California business or rental properties are generating income, those will still be taxed by California.

Don't Burn that Mortgage

Many older Americans assume that they have to have their house paid off when they retire. Perhaps this is a hangover from Depression-era thinking, or perhaps it's simply an emotional decision—some people feel better knowing they don't owe anything on their real estate. But don't automatically assume that your house mortgage should be paid off the day you retire.

If you owe some money to the bank for a mortgage, you might want to ask what the after-tax cost of borrowing money is for you. Let me give you an example. Let's say you have a 6 percent mortgage, and you are paying taxes at a 25 percent tax rate. Your after-tax cost of borrowing, therefore, is 4 ½ percent. Now, with the risk posture you've taken on your investments, what's your expected rate of return? If it's higher than 4 ½ percent, why would you want to pay off the loan? From a financial point of view, you come out ahead by keeping your mortgage in place.

But finances, as we've seen repeatedly through this book, have as much to do with emotion as with anything else. Some people just feel better knowing that they don't owe any money. They may want to pay off their mortgage simply because they want to reduce their monthly costs. But if you've got a few million in assets, there's no harm in leaving a half-million-dollar mortgage out there. It's not going to hurt you, and it certainly can make an important difference for you financially.

If you don't like to travel that much, then you can choose a place that's so attractive that other people are going to want to come to visit you. We have close friends in Aspen who are not crazy about travel. But all their friends want to come to Aspen, to ski in the winter and play golf in the summer. So that may be the most important criterion of all: Where would you like to live so that your friends will be lining up to come visit you?

Make No Mistake …

There's no law that says that you've got to stay in the same house in retirement as you did during your income-producing and child-raising years. You've earned the right to go and do wherever and whatever you want—so go there and do it! It's worth spending a little bit of time exploring, first on paper and then with vacations and short-term rentals, exactly what your ideal days would be like and where you would go if you wanted to live those dreams.

You really have earned the right to live the way you want. Don't let fear or inertia bog you down. Get cracking—and start packing!

8

Mistake #4: Settling for Less

Few successful people I meet in their forties and beyond accomplished much of anything without setting goals. I'm sure there are some lucky people out there, but such people are few and far between. I'm extremely goal-oriented and always have been. I have a strong sense that you are the same way, too. If so, we're kindred spirits, and we're not alone.

You may be familiar with the study of the Yale University class from the early 1960s, indicating that the 3 percent of the class with written goals enjoyed, by their twenty-fifth reunion, a net worth equal to the net worth of the remaining 97 percent of their classmates. Goals, especially written ones, are extremely powerful. They give us something to shoot for. They give us a way to measure our success. They inspire us to move forward, to roll out of bed on dark, cold mornings when we would much rather hit the snooze button, and to go forth and do great things, for ourselves and the world. Goals get you going.

In his book *Wealth Without Risk,* Charles J. Givens makes a fascinating point that it initially takes us ten units of effort in order to achieve one unit of results. If we are dedicated to our work, however, the ratio eventually shifts, to the point where one unit of effort creates ten units of results. Chances are that you have experienced this same phenomenon yourself, since you are in a position to retire with a tidy sum of money in the bank, successful investments, and a rosy financial future ahead of you.

If I may be so bold, I'd like to make a further surmise about the nature of the goals you set. I'll bet they were big goals. I'll bet they were—in the phrase popularized in Jim Collins's book *Good to Great: Why Some Companies Make the Leap … and Others Don't*—BHAGs: Big Hairy Audacious Goals. You most likely set yourself these sorts of goals during college or your early training. You have always expected much from yourself, and as a result, you have accomplished much, and you have a great deal about which you can be proud. Big Hairy Audacious Goals drive us forward. As the motivator Tony Robbins points out, nobody ever felt a great pull of motivation by the need to just pay the bills. The reason you're reading this book is because your vision of what was possible for you was large, and as a result of dreaming very big dreams, you have accomplished great results. Don't stop now!

Goals Work for Everyone

This is the case regardless of whether you came from a comfortable financial background, a working-class family, or even dire poverty. Inherited wealth can cripple the individual, while the lack of money in one's childhood can be a great motivator. Two people from the same sort of family, financial, or socioeconomic background can end up in entirely different places, ultimately because of the goals they set for themselves and how true they remained to setting those goals.

Earl Nightingale, the father of the modern-day personal development movement, tells the story of two sons with an alcoholic father. One son became an alcoholic. "What could I do," he said, "coming from a background like that?" The other son avoided alcohol completely and went on to become a great success in every department of his life. "What else could I do," he explained, "coming from a background like that?"

Why do some succeed and others fail? Why is it that nineteen out of twenty people who reach the age of sixty-five are either dead or dead broke? There are many explanations, but ultimately, I believe it comes down to the fact that some people set high expectations for themselves in their lives, and "went for it" with everything they had, while others did not.

So if you and I see the great power of goal setting in our financial and professional lives, there's a mystery we have to unravel. Why do so many people who do well financially not opt for setting goals in the other areas of their lives?

And why do so many people who set goals in their financial and professional lives cease setting goals once they reach the magic age of retirement?

I can understand that you might want to retire from work after all these years. What I can't understand is why successful people would want to retire from goal setting. The years prior to retirement and your retirement years themselves are perfect times for applying goal setting to all areas of one's life, not just the financial. Goals work in all areas! I understand the logic of the counter-argument: When your career ends, why do you need to keep setting goals? But when your career ends, you now have the chance to experience a sense of balance and fulfillment that eludes many individuals during their working careers. You've made it financially, and for that I congratulate you. Now what do you want to make of the rest of your life? Where do you want to point your life, now that you'll have so much more control over your time and daily activities?

Goals Across the Board

Here's a list of areas where you can set goals for the remainder of your life. I hesitate to use the phrase "the rest of your life" because for most people in your position, retirement and "rest" are not the same thing. Retirement used to conjure up images of an elderly man sitting in a rocking chair on a porch, a gold watch securely fastened around his wrist. But what's the good of having a gold watch if it doesn't matter what time it is, and it doesn't matter what time it is because you don't have anywhere to go? I'm sure that's not the notion of retirement that you have in mind.

Here is a list of areas in which you can elect to set goals for the next year, the next three years, the next five years, and the remainder of your life:

- Family relationships
- Home environment
- Physical goals (health, exercise, nutrition)
- Social goals (friendship and organizations)
- Educational goals

- Spiritual goals

- Financial goals

I put financial goals at the bottom of the list not because they're unimportant—they're very important. It's just that I want you to broaden your thinking. Just as you set and achieved—and most likely exceeded—financial goals in your life, I want you to start thinking about setting goals in *all* areas. In terms of your family relationships—your marriage, your relationships with your children and grandchildren—I want to suggest that goals can be extremely powerful.

If you've been working forty or even sixty hours a week, you and your spouse are in for a big jolt when you begin spending so much time together. (In traditional marriages, this is often more frightening for the wife than the husband, because the husband will be invading and hanging around her domain *all day long*.) What do you want your relationship to be like now? What do you want your marriage to be like? I titled this chapter—and this Mistake—"Settling for Less" because that's what so many of us do. You didn't settle for less in your finances, so why would you settle for anything less than the optimal in any other aspect of your life, especially at a point when you have the time, the money, and the motivation to maximize your happiness and satisfaction?

I wouldn't suggest that you write down a single sentence like "I want to have a great relationship with my wife (or husband)." Instead, I'd like you to get much more specific. What should the nature of communication between you and your spouse be like? When you spend time together, what are you going to do? What activities will you pursue jointly? But don't make the mistake of thinking that now that you're retired, you will find just the right activity that interests both you and your spouse.

Wayne Sotile is a prominent clinical psychologist, author of *Thriving with Heart Disease*, and a close friend. He has counseled couples for thirty years and we bring him in to meet our clients when circumstances so warrant. He told me that the process of trying to find that "magical couple experience" is a leading cause that gets couples to see him for marriage counseling. He says if you both can find that one activity, it's like hitting the lottery. The reality is that you might share a passion for the same thing and you might not. Don't drag your spouse onto the golf course to try to get her to discover her hidden passion for golf. And don't make him sit through Wagner's Ring Cycle just because you love opera. Ideally, there will be some areas that interest you both. Maybe travel is something you can agree on. Give yourselves permission to develop different interests.

The bigger issue is this: How will you treat each other, now that you have so much more time together? What steps might you need to take, as individuals or as a couple, in order to improve the quality of your communication, intimacy, or any other aspect of your life? Not every problem can be solved by a little blue pill.

Be specific. You've already set big, hairy, audacious financial goals, and you exceeded them. What goals would you like to set—and exceed—for your marriage or your relationship? Or maybe you're living alone at this point and you would like to enter into a relationship or a marriage. Put your goals down on paper. You've already proven to yourself the power of goal setting in your work and financial life. Now put that same power to work here.

The same goes for your home environment. Remember the conversation at the beginning of the previous chapter. Don't settle for less by staying put if the places you want to go and the things you like to do are located elsewhere. Don't let inertia keep you tied to one spot. Get out there and see what life has to offer. You've paid your dues! So now the question becomes this: What do you want your home, or homes, to look like? How do you want them furnished? Are you happy with what you have, or is it time to start fresh? You can get decorating or architectural magazines and start cutting out pictures, so that you can visualize your new way of living. Whether it's remodeling or redecorating your current home to meet your new needs or thinking through the places to which you might relocate, get busy. Don't settle. Decide what you want, write it down, and make it happen.

You and Your Body

When it comes to physical goals, we all know what the doctor is going to tell us: Eat better, eat less, and exercise more. But a vague sense of "I've got to lose five pounds" (or "I've got to lose forty-five pounds") generally leads to a sense of "I'll start next week." When you've got written goals about how you want your body to look, things change. Don't be afraid to write down what you want to weigh, what you want your cholesterol to be, what you want your blood pressure to be, and all the other specifics about what optimal health means to you.

Today more than ever, the way we age is a function of the choices we make. There are fifty-year-olds who are exhausted with life and ready to throw themselves on the scrap heap, and there are seventy-year-olds lining up for marathons and triathlons. The old, limited notions of what an "older person" can do and how old you have to be to earn that label are rapidly falling away.

Get a personal trainer—you can afford it. Get to the gym, or build a gym into your home. Or just get out and walk, run, bicycle, or ski. But do so in an organized fashion. Use that same goal-setting part of your brain that brought you so much financial success to bring you the body that you would really like to have. You'll be pleased … and so will your spouse. And if you've got children and grandchildren, wouldn't you like to be able to enjoy them, travel to them or with them, and be a part of their lives for more years? That's why it's so important to set physical goals for yourself.

Where appropriate, we bring in a personal trainer to meet our clients, if they so desire. Incidentally, our firm is unique in that we don't pretend we have all the answers. We know something about retirement, but we turn to experts in the fields of psychology, law, fitness, nutrition and other areas as appropriate. We preach balance, and we believe that wisdom comes from many sources—not just our own great minds!

Setting Social Goals

Social goals are next. When I talk about social goals, I mean asking yourself about the quality and quantity of friendships you would like to enjoy in coming years. Men, especially during their working years, don't always have the time or even the inclination for friendships. Sure, you might have a golfing foursome, but how deeply do you really get into each other's lives? How much do you even know about each other? Or perhaps a weekly round of golf is something that your work schedule simply did not permit. If so, you're not alone.

Now that you're becoming free from the awesome time commitment that your career has demanded, whom do you want to be with? What kind of people would you like to get to know? Where do you find them? What about old friends? What about getting in touch with the people that you most liked years ago? Often, we drift away from people not because we stopped liking them, but because we stopped having time or occasion to see them.

Write down your social goals—who you want to be with, how often, doing what, where, and why. Life really is about being with people. So don't let inertia or drifting away keep you from invigorating or rediscovering the bonds of friendship you've enjoyed in the past.

Educate yourself

Educational goals keep you mentally sharp. It's all about keeping those synapses in the brain firing away! Experts say that the best thing to do when you retire is to learn a new language—and when you master that one, learn another one! The mind is a muscle like any other in your body, and the same rule applies: Use it or lose it.

What have you always wanted to learn, but never had time for? Now is the time. When you were younger, you might have been debating whether to earn an MBA or get your license in real estate. Why not learn Italian? That way, you can explore the deepest regions of Umbria or Tuscany and speak the language. What a great adventure that will be!

Goals for the Spirit

The subject of spiritual goals is an extremely personal matter, and I'm not here to tell you whether to believe or what to believe. I will say that individuals who have taken the time to explore the spiritual side of life are often much more content and at peace than those who have not. If you've never had the time or inclination to explore your spiritual side, there's no time like the present. A trip to your local bookstore will give you all the materials you need to start a new passion for understanding your spiritual nature. What would your goal be in this area? Write that down, too.

Don't Forget the Money!

While we've been talking about all these other areas of your life (some of them seemingly esoteric) as fertile ground for goal setting, don't forget about your financial life. Just because you've retired doesn't mean that your money has! As we've mentioned in earlier chapters, the time frame for financial growth is not demarcated by your retirement date. Instead, your horizon equals your lifespan. Continue to set goals for your financial life. You may not be working, but your money can be working for you.

Where would you like to be financially at age sixty-five? At age seventy? At age seventy-five? What would you like to leave to your children? To your church? To your community? What kinds of charitable trusts or other vehicles do you need to put in place now in order to make those desires happen down the road? Financial planning for an individual like you has always meant financial dreaming. You've never been satisfied with where you were. That's why you've gotten where you are, so why stop now?

The Goal Behind the Goal

What's this all about? It's not about creating busywork to distract you from the aging process or anything foolish like that. Instead, what I'm proposing is that you take control of your destiny by creating a vision of a high quality of life for yourself and those around you, right up to the end of your days. None of us wants to take the inevitable downturn toward ill health that old age typically calls to mind. The more active you are in mind and body, the longer you can reasonably expect to enjoy life to its fullest.

To an increasing extent, the way we age is a choice. You had a better working life than most people because you made a decision to set goals to achieve that life. So why not do the same thing in retirement? You don't have to fall apart mentally or physically, especially if you know where you want to go and what you want to accomplish. Open your mind to all these different goal categories and you'll see just what you're capable of.

Three Sets of Goals

I advocate setting short-range, intermediate, and long-range goals in each of the above categories.

Let's say you decide that you need to shed forty pounds. That may sound impossible, but broken into smaller steps, you can finally reach the larger goal. You might set a goal of being forty pounds lighter with better muscle tone three years from now. This allows you to create an intermediate goal of dropping fifteen pounds this year and leads you to create the short-range goal of developing the habit of working out three days a week. One goal leads to the next.

Picture yourself three years out looking back where you are now. What has to happen during that time for you to get where you want to be, for you to be satisfied with your progress? What strengths do you possess that will get you to those goals? What weaknesses will keep you from them? And if you could accomplish a goal in this area, what else would you accomplish in your life?

During our working lives, we might not have had the time for exercise. I see many people who are in much better health and enjoying a higher level of fitness in retirement than they ever did while they were working. The boomer generation may be a little more attuned to physical fitness than those that preceded it, but all of us could probably benefit from an extra trip to the gym. Again, we believe a personal trainer is one of the best investments our clients—or anyone—could make.

True Success

There's a quotation I keep on my desktop, and I study it regularly: "Success is not necessarily defined by money or position but by happiness in our daily lives and growth in our human potential." This is the time to maximize your human potential. Up through the 1950s, work was everything. Then the Beatles came along and sang to our generation, "All You

Need Is Love." The pendulum is swinging to the middle now. We need both of these things in equal amounts. We need to contribute, we need to grow, and we need to love. And the best way to achieve anything in life is to set goals so that we know exactly where we want to head.

Goal setting has a wonderful unintended benefit: You'll feel younger and more alive. Anything that you think about grows. If you focus your mind on the fact that you are aging, those thoughts just accelerate the process. Instead, think about what's on your goal list and what you can do right now, today, and take yourself a step closer to accomplishing some or all of them.

Does Life "Happen"?

Some people believe that "life happens" to them and there's nothing they can do about anything. This negative attitude is infectious. It's in our culture, it's in our entertainment, and it's in much of the water cooler conversation you hear in the workplace. I don't buy it, and neither should you. You weren't passive in your work life. Why would you want to get passive now about the rest of your life? The only creator of your retirement is *you*. Get firmly in your mind the idea that you can create a phenomenal life, unlike anything you've ever experienced before. When you get that firmly in your mind, with passion, that idea will trickle through your subconscious to make that great life possible.

Affirmations

I know you're thinking I'm getting a little Left Coast, but let me assure you that I've got my feet planted firmly in the soil of North Carolina. But I do want to introduce you to a concept with which you may not be familiar. It has to do with affirmations. To "affirm" something is to make it firm, solid, *real*. You might have used affirmations when you were on your way to the top. I'd like to suggest that you use affirmations to make your new sets of retirement goals come true.

The key to affirmations is to keep things in present tense and to start each statement with the word "I." If you say, "I want a new car," you're not really focused on the new car. You're focused on the wanting! And whatever you focus on, you get more of! A better affirmation: "I love my new car!" "I love my new vacation house!"

Here are some other powerful affirmations:

"I enjoy great health and great relationships."

"I have a great time with my spouse and my kids."

"I've got all the money I need for a fantastic retirement."

"I enjoy great health and fitness."

When you construct affirmations like these for yourself, and you repeat them regularly—some authors say that you need to repeat an affirmation at least fifteen times a day in order to lock it into your brain—something miraculous happens. Your subconscious, the 85 percent of your mind to which your conscious mind is the gatekeeper, cannot distinguish between reality and whatever you say is reality. So if you tell your subconscious, "I enjoy great health and fitness," your subconscious mind will come up with ways to make that statement true. Suddenly you'll find yourself signing up for a gym membership, hiring a personal trainer, or going for a long walk without knowing exactly why or how you got there.

By contrast, failing to give yourself positive affirmations sets you up to be the victim of negative affirmations, such as "I'm getting old and there's nothing I can do about it." Ever told yourself that canard? I hope not! Because if you do, your subconscious mind will find ways to make that true for you. Every one of the seventy trillion cells in your body is listening to you at all times, taking cues from your conscious mind and what you tell yourself, consciously or unconsciously. Make the right choices—feed your mind as thoughtfully as you feed your body. You know that you're not going to have a great day if you have junk food for breakfast. So why indulge in junk thought?

Make No Mistake …

Goals worked beautifully for you while you were on your way to the top. Now that you're at the top, there's another pinnacle you can reach. It takes more than money to get there. It takes true life balance. And that's now yours to achieve. As Nike says, "Just Do It!"

9

Mistake #3: Spending Too Much

Cash flow is where the rubber meets the road when you're in retirement. Since it occurs daily, many people don't focus on the long-term aspects. This is true of spending patterns, considering inflation, gifting to your kids, and has a huge impact on how you construct your portfolio. I could probably write a short book on just this one subject, but let me give you the CliffsNotes version.

"We'll do just fine on $150,000 a year," the client confidently assures me.

Twelve months later, we sit down again together.

"We thought we could get by on $150,000," the client says, with a slightly sheepish expression on his face. "We spent $180,000? Really?"

It's not that hard to go over budget in your retirement years, especially if you've never really had to deal with a budget in your adult life. Most of the people with whom I work earn substantial amounts of income, and they rarely have to make choices while they are still working. They can't go completely crazy, of course—no solid gold faucets in the guest bathroom or Olympic-sized pools filled with Perrier. But by and large, they can afford pretty much anything within reason, and as their income increases year after year, so does their spending.

And then retirement comes, and with it, a whole new financial reality: They're not making money anymore. Their money might be making money, but they aren't. What's a retiree to do?

It's critically important for individuals who have retired or are contemplating retirement to get used to the idea that they have to rein in their spending so that they don't end up outliving their money, or even coming close to doing so. The people with whom I work—individuals with net worths of typically $1 million to $5 million, excluding the value of their home or homes—tend to feel that they are well-off. And they are well-off—but they aren't superrich. They can afford to live nicely in their retirement years, but they have to pay careful attention to where the money goes. They've got to make their money last.

Man Does Not Live by Yield Alone

Here's the most crucial error I see on the part of retirees who are managing their money: They don't understand that investments do not need to yield the cash flow they desire. Let me explain what I mean, since almost every single retiree gets caught up on this point.

Retirees decide what kind of cash they think they need, so they try to position their portfolios to get their investments to yield that amount. Let's say, for example, that Joe is worth $3 million, and he wants to live on $150,000 a year. This means that he needs to make 5 percent on his money. So what does Joe do? He takes a look at what dividends are paying on stocks, and he sees that the S&P average yield is around 2 percent. That's no good. Aha! Bonds pay around 5 percent! That's the way to go. Joe, trying to make his $150,000 solely on the yield from his investment, has gotten chased over to bonds.

In year one, Joe has invested $3 million in bonds, the bonds pay 5 percent, and Joe's got his $150,000. So far, so good.

The problem is that Joe will be retired for a long, long time—or so he hopes. Yet Joe has all of his money in one of the most conservative investments possible: high-quality bonds. Due to inflation, Joe is destined to go broke. In year two, he won't need just $150,000 to maintain the same standard of living. Assuming 3 percent inflation, Joe will need $154,500. This means that he has to reduce, ever so slightly, the quality of bonds in his portfolio, so as to make 5.2 percent on his $3 million. The following year, inflation will eat further away at Joe's buying power, so he'll need to earn just a little bit more. The following year, even more, and so on.

It's now year five. Due to the ravages of inflation, Joe will find himself needing increasingly more income to maintain the same lifestyle he enjoyed in year one. Instead of a 5 percent return, Joe needs almost 6 percent. How is he going to get it, since he feels he is committed to living off the yield of his investments and not touching the principal?

His only choice is lower-quality bonds—and, dare I say, junk bonds. Now he'll be earning what he needs currently, but the bonds he's bought have a higher risk of defaulting, putting his $3 million—and the rest of his retirement—at serious risk. And if you think it's risky trying to get 6 percent out of a portfolio heavily weighted toward bonds, in the future it just won't be possible to earn enough interest to offset inflation. We could say that Joe is skidding off the yield curve.

Before long, Joe will have no choice but to eat into his principal, with no growth to offset that nibbling. He's actually headed for a geometric progression: The more time that passes, the more principal he must spend just to maintain his standard of living. This is not a happy situation.

Inflated Opinions

Joe has made the same mistake that many retirees make: He has failed to factor inflation into his retirement plans. We never know exactly what inflation will be, but we typically build 3 percent into our models for our clients. Inflation is part of our economic system, and a little bit is actually a good thing. That's the basic struggle that the Fed faces—they can't allow inflation to get too high, but by the same token, they can't afford to let it drop too low. Declining prices actually harm the economy, and they hurt the pocketbooks of retirees, too.

You might think that dropping prices are a dream come true. But the problem is that when you're retired, you're living on your investments. In deflationary times, the value of your investments drop. The whole economy staggers. People don't want to buy something new now when they can get it cheaper the following month. Ben Bernanke and the other members of the Federal Reserve Board would have to drastically cut interest rates just to reignite the economy. So a little bit of inflation is actually good for the system.

The only person who wins in deflationary times is the individual deeply invested in cash or bonds. You're lending your money out, and when you get it back, it will have even more buying power. It's not really an investment strategy that I would recommend. If you think that we're going to have any level of inflation at all (and just about anybody who studies these matters feels that way) then the wisest course is to own things that go up in value during inflationary periods, such as stocks and real estate. Ideally, you want to have a diversified, balanced portfolio, not too heavily weighted in either stocks or bonds. As we have discussed earlier in this book, you want to align your portfolio with your volatility comfort level.

So if failing to factor inflation is a mistake that you want to avoid, are you done? Do you have your retirement financial model all sewn up at this point?

Not really. There's yet another factor that most retirees fail to take into account.

What the Heck?

This is the statement that often precedes many large financial decisions. "What the heck? Let's go to Italy for a month. We've got the money!" Or "What the heck? Let's get that new car. Ours is kind of a clunker, isn't it?" Or "What the heck? Let's pick up the tab for a big family vacation for all our kids and grandkids. They'll all remember it for the rest of their lives!"

I'm highlighting here the fact that when it comes to spending in retirement, you can absolutely expect the unexpected. There's always going to be some big-ticket item that you didn't factor into your month-by-month budgeting that will tear your financial blueprints asunder. The moment when people make these big spending decisions often comes upon them so quickly that they don't even know what hit them. The only time they realize that they have far exceeded their annual spending target is when they sit down with their financial advisor.

You take an impromptu trip to the Riviera. Or you get hit with a big bill because you had to fix the roof. Or your car broke down. Whatever the reason, that $150,000 you intended to spend can easily shoot up to $180,000—or more. Don't lock yourself into a cash-flow pattern with no wiggle room to it. At the same time, keep in mind that you may not be able to spend with the same freedom you enjoyed while you were bringing in a regular paycheck.

Selling Discipline

When you retire, you'll be a net seller of investments ... for the rest of your life. If you're going to be selling more than you're buying, then you need to become an extremely disciplined seller. You need what we call "sell discipline," some kind of strategy so that you can avoid selling into a down market, or because everybody else is in a panic and you get caught up in it.

Let's say that you need some cash flow and the stock market is down. What's your plan?

For most people, it's simple: sell stock. There's only one problem with that. In one out of every three years on average, the market goes down. If you think back to the 1990s, we had a long period of time where the market only went up. This developed a sense of overconfidence—dare I say, irrational exuberance—on the part of many investors. The next three years, starting in the year 2000, saw the market tumble. Six years up, three years down—that works out to the ratio I shared with you a moment earlier—in one out of every three years, the market is down.

The only problem is that you never know what next year is going to be. This means you must develop a strategy for dealing with the fact that you may have unexpected needs for cash flow without resorting to selling in a down market.

The Old-School Method

If your father were a financial advisor, here's what he'd tell you to do. Let's say you've got a portfolio of 60 percent stocks and 40 percent bonds. You need to raise money, because it's your philosophy to take money off the table and put it into your money market account every six or twelve months. But the market's down.

The old-school approach that your father would use would be to take the money from the bonds side. Now you're seventy to thirty, stocks to bonds. You're letting your fixed-income side slide down a little bit. That's okay, because you wouldn't want to "sell ratably," or sell equal percentages of stocks and bonds. If you did, you'd be selling stocks at a price lower than what you bought them, and losing money in the stock market doesn't strike you—or your father—as a good idea.

Here's a neater way to accomplish the goal of providing sufficient cash flow for your entire retirement.

So Good, You'll Stagger

It's tough to make one portfolio do two different things—grow *and* spin off enough money to meet your cash flow needs. So I suggest to my clients that they create a second account from which they will draw their income. This income-producing account will comprise staggered maturity bonds or CDs. It will be your plan to live off the principal and the interest in this account. Let's see how it works.

Instead of thinking six to twelve months at a time, I want you to think about biting off five years at a time. Let's say you've got that same $3 million, and you think you can live on $150,000 a year plus your Social Security benefits and that you've built a contingency factor into your budget.

If you're going to need $150,000 (plus 3 percent inflation) a year for five years, then this account has to total about $700,000. Here's a schedule of what this might look like, based on an actual laddered bond portfolio we worked out for one of our clients in mid-2006:

Bond Amount	Description	2007 Interest
$135,000	4.375% coupon, due 12/31/07	$5,906
$144,000	3.375% coupon, due 12/15/08	$4,860
$155,000	3.50% coupon, due 12/15/09	$5,425
$ 166,000	4.375% coupon, due 12/15/10	$7,262
	4% Interest on average Money Market balance	$ 2,481
	Total income	$25,934

During the first year of your five-year plan, live off the cash in this account of $124,066 plus the interest of $25,934 which magically gets you to your $150,000 target. When that year comes to a close, cash in the one-year bond, and with the interest income on the other three bonds plus your interest income, there's your money for that year ($154,500 with 3 percent inflation). When that year ends, your two-year bond will be maturing, so you cash that one in and live on that money plus the interest. Ditto the three-year bond for the fourth year of this process, and the four-year bond for the fifth year. In short, you've provided safety and security for yourself by coming up with exactly the amount of money you need in each of the first five years of your retirement. Your cash flow needs are very comfortably met.

What about the rest of the money?

Time To Grow

You took $700,000 and set it aside for your five-year cash flow account. That leaves you with $2.3 million, and a period of five years in order to let that $2.3 million grow back to the original $3 million. I'll do the math for you: You need your money to grow by 30 percent. The good news is that you've got five years to do it. Even before you think about compound interest, you only need a gain of 6 percent a year on your investment to reach that target. But hang on! You don't want to just grow back to $3 million! You'll need to realize some additional growth so you can keep giving yourself a raise each year to offset inflation.

Now you have a selling discipline. Let's say that after three years, the stock market has a pretty good run and it's up 40 percent. It's time to trim your stock side, now that it's back over the $3 million dollar level, and pull out another $700,000 (plus what you'll need for inflation) to cover your second five-year plan. Keep in mind that you're only three years into your first five-year plan, so now you have seven years to earn that 30+ percent all over again, so you can get your third ladder of bonds. You've got money growing nicely in one portfolio, you've got no pressure to take money off the table for cash flow in a down market, and you've got a nice, steady bond portfolio giving you all the cash you need to live nicely. You've got it made.

Making Your Money Go Further

In an earlier chapter, we discussed the mistake of allowing inertia to dictate where and how you live. This concept of managing your cash flow ties back to the concept of relocating, not just for a superior quality of life, but in order to maximize the value of your retirement dollars. There's a scene in the Marx Brothers film *A Night at the Opera,* in which Groucho and Chico whittle a thousand-dollar-a-week opera contract down to a mere ten dollars a week for the singer Chico ostensibly represents.

"Can you live in New York on ten dollars a week?" Chico asks dubiously.

"Of course!" Groucho exclaims. "As long as you don't eat!"

Few of the clients with whom I work are trying to figure out how to get by in New York on ten dollars a week. But the fact is that the $150,000 we've been talking about plus, say, another $30,000 in Social Security, or $180,000 in total goes a lot further in some parts of the country than it does in others. You definitely want to take the cost of living into account as you consider your financial future and where and how you want to live. Let's say you live in Los Angeles, a very expensive place, indeed. A hundred eighty thousand dollars a year buys you a decent standard of living. But transplant yourself to virtually anyplace else in the country, and you can live like a pasha on much less than 180K. What to do?

If you live in an expensive part of the country, ask yourself what features or benefits your region offers that you might be able to replicate someplace else. For example, some people live in Southern California because, as they like to say, "There's nothing to shovel." But you could live in Texas, Florida, Georgia, or a number of other states and never see a snowflake. If it's the cultural life that keeps you tied to Manhattan, you may discover that there are other places in the United States offering as rich or almost as rich a cultural life at a fraction of Big Apple prices. Maybe one of those less expensive places might have some appeal for you.

I had two clients who lived in Los Angeles, and they were tired of the urban lifestyle. They sold their L.A. home, took their money off the table in that potentially topsy-turvy real estate market, and bought a beautiful farm in Illinois. They're about as happy as any couple I've ever seen.

Thanks, Dad!

As long as we're talking about not messing up cash flow, let's talk about the importance of not messing up the cash flow of your children or grandchildren. To begin this discussion, let's keep in mind what estate tax tells us. After your $2 million exemption, your total net worth is subject to estate tax. If you're in this financial grouping, then the last thing you want to do is lie on your deathbed thinking about just how much of your hard-earned money is going to the I.R.S. What do you want to do about that?

If you're like many people at this financial level, you're probably already making cash gifts to your heirs. Tax law currently permits the gifting of $12,000 a year from each donor to each recipient, tax-free to both parties. If you're married and your child is married, this means that you can transfer $48,000 a year to your child and his or her spouse, tax-free. This reduces your eventual estate tax burden and gets some money into the hands of your kids.

This transfer is usually preceded by this caveat from adult parent to adult child: "We can give you the money this year, but don't count on it happening every year. We may not be in a position to do this down the line. I hope you'll do something smart with it, like investing it, buying some real estate, or putting it into your business. I know you'll do the right thing."

Unfortunately, your kids now have $48,000 tax-free reasons why they shouldn't work as hard. They'd have to go out and earn almost $100,000 to equate the largesse that you just bestowed upon them. So you're sapping their initiative, and, despite all the good intentions of the Talk, they're most likely *not* going to do something smart with the money. Oh, they might pay off a car loan or buy a new car, but you and I both know that free money generally gets frittered away. In financial planning talk, that gift has been incorporated into their cash flow.

Some young people use this money as a means of paying their mortgage. In financial-planning jargon, such individuals are living beyond their means. You're giving them the money with the best of intentions, but they're getting hurt because they may not know how to handle the sudden burst of money you just forked over.

The real trouble comes a few years down the road, when you've retired and the $48,000 a year that you've been handing out to each of your kids seems like a lot of money. Suddenly you and your spouse start thinking about all the things that the two of you could do if you hung on to that $48,000 (times the number of children and grandchildren) that you've been doling out. So now comes the Other Talk. "Your mom and I have been thinking. Now that we're retired, we can't give you that whole $48,000 anymore. But I've been telling you every year that this could come to pass, so I know you're not going to be shattered by the news."

Wrong! They're shattered. They're *very* shattered. They've been counting on that money. Things move rapidly from "Thanks, Dad!" to "How could you do this to me?"

I know you mean well by transferring all that cash to your offspring. But ultimately, you may be doing them—and your relationship with them—far more harm than good.

The most depressing client for whom I've ever worked is an individual who lives in a fantastic home at the base of one of the most beautiful ski resorts in North America. He's totally miserable. He's also filthy rich. The reason he's miserable is not because he's got too much money. It's because he's got too little challenge. He was handed so much money by his parents at such an early age that he doesn't know what to do with himself. He has no incentive to contribute to society, because there's nothing on earth that could possibly pay him as well as taking a Jacuzzi or a nap. He literally makes more money sleeping than most of us will ever make with our eyes open.

Money isn't the root of all evil. *Love* of money is the root of all evil and *free money* is a close second. So be very careful about dumping free money on people whose initiatives may be sapped by your generosity.

In Family We Trust

There are ways to pass money to kids and grandkids without hurting them. You can establish a family trust, partnership, limited-liability company, or some other vehicle that allows you to relinquish ownership of the asset without giving up control. It works this way.

Let's say that Mr. and Ms. Smith opened up the Smith Family Partnership. The Smiths are the general partners. The Smith children are the limited partners. The older Smiths use their annual gift exclusion to make donations into the Smith Family Partnership. The children will get the money one day, but not soon enough for them to mess up their lives.

Such arrangements also have the flexibility to permit distributions in case of special situations. If the Smith kids ran into unusual medical expenses, the Smith parents can make a distribution to their kids, who, after all, are limited partners in the Smith Family Partnership. Through the Smith Family Partnership, the Smiths can also pay for education, a down payment on a home, or anything else they choose. But since the Smith children and grandchildren don't have control of the money, they don't have anything sapping their cash flow. How smart is that?

As I write these words, I'm reminded of something that the wife of a surgeon told me. "I just want to figure out what we should do when my husband gets his next raise in salary," she said. "I don't want that amount to trigger an inadvertent increase in lifestyle."

Ah, there it is. The dreaded I.I.L., "Inadvertent Increase in Lifestyle." We do tend to increase our spending at a rate that often exceeds our ability to pay. While this can be a costly mistake while we are still working, it can be a fatal error in our retirement years.

Make No Mistake …

Fund your retirement, but be careful about situations of overspending—whether it's you, your spouse, your children, or your grandchildren who are wielding that American Express card. Maybe it's time to leave home without it.

10

Mistake #2: Thinking It's Gonna Be Easy

No job. No kids. No boss. No worries.

Right?

Wrong.

If you think the transition from your working life to retirement is going to be easy, think again.

It's time to face the facts—you are about to go through one of the greatest upheavals ever, touching every facet of your life. Think about it: You're going from a place where you are respected and admired (or, perhaps, feared!) to a situation in which no one knows who you are.

"Isn't that Joe?" you might hear, as you go for a stroll on your first day of retirement. "Didn't he used to be Dr. Green?"

You're still Dr. Green, but without the office to go to, the work to do, the patients to see, or the people to supervise. A lot of your status—and self-definition—has vanished overnight.

Not going to the office means a lot more than status, though. Most working people derive the overwhelming amount of their social contact from their workplace. You can see a great game on TV on Tuesday night, but if you're retired, with whom are you going to discuss it on Wednesday morning? Or if you hit a hole in one on Sunday, whom are you going to tell on Monday? Suddenly, a large chunk of the social interplay you have enjoyed for decades has disappeared before your very eyes.

The same thing is true of intellectual stimulation. Chances are that you have worked for decades in a profession that requires constant study in order to keep up with the latest trends, research, legal changes, or other twists and turns. Guess what? As a retiree, you're no longer expected to keep up with that massive information flow that you've been complaining about. So one of your most important processes—the studying and implementing of new intellectual material—has gone, too, and you'll miss it. Ironic, isn't it?

You've lost much of your status, you've lost much of your social world, you've lost a good part of your intellectual challenges, and you don't really have anywhere particular to get to. So where do you go? Or more accurately, where do you stay?

If you're like most retirees, the answer is simple: home. Only one slight problem here. Your spouse has devoted the last several decades to having the home exactly the way she likes it. (Bear with me through this one politically incorrect paragraph.) The newly retired husband more often than not finds himself in conflict with his wife's patterns and routines, and this can put an enormous amount of strain on a marriage. When you're working, you might have seen your spouse early in the morning for a short while and then again in the evening, on weekends, and during vacations. But now, you're available for lunch, brunch, afternoon snack, and all the hours in between mealtimes, as well. The problem is that *she* may not be available. She's got her own life, and during your formerly working hours, it doesn't include you, buster!

Serious as a Heart Attack

If I've painted a picture of retirement that sounds anything other than idyllic, then I've represented the situation with great accuracy. Retirement can be the most wonderful time of your life. You finally have all the time in the world to do everything that you want to do—you're no longer weighed down by work responsibilities, the challenge of raising children, the stress of paying off a mortgage, and all the other activities and events that occupy us from the day we graduate until the day we retire. Now you've got time to play all the golf you've ever wanted to play, to travel, and to read, or simply to sleep in. But unless you've prepared properly for the transition from your working life to your new life, you are putting yourself in the way of serious trouble.

How serious? Within the first twelve months after retirement, the three most common problems faced by those who fail to prepare are heart attacks, depression, and divorce. That's why I say I'm serious as a heart attack about your need to prepare properly before your transition to retirement. Most people get the money part right—they figure out budget and cash flow issues, or at least they have a starting point, as we've seen in previous chapters. But your retirement isn't just about money. It's about what you're going to do and how you're going to live.

Dr. Wayne Sotile, the clinical psychologist whom I mentioned earlier, tells new retirees who have heart attacks, "I'm going to put you on a long list of people I know who have had heart attacks in the first twelve months after retirement." The usual reason for heart attacks, I believe, is that the human body simply doesn't know what to do with all the energy that used to be diverted to work, commuting, and other such issues. Those who don't have heart attacks often become depressed because they don't know what to do with themselves, and that explains the substantial jump in the prescription of anti-depression medication amidst the newly retired. And finally, couples counseling and the divorce rate skyrocket in that first year. All the issues that couples have, that might have simmered quietly over the decades, can no longer be avoided as members of a couple realize that their partners are not the people with whom they want to spend the rest of their lives.

So how do you avoid these problems?

Not a River in Egypt

The first step is to come out of denial over the fact that the transition to retirement is going to be easy. Let's face the facts—it won't be. If you plan how you're going to live your post-retirement years as carefully as you planned the means by which you are going to fund them, you'll be all right. If not, you are putting yourself at risk of truly life-threatening and happiness-threatening issues.

Let's talk about marriage. In a traditional setting, the wife is the one who sacrificed the most over the years. She was stuck at home raising the kids. This is not to denigrate the importance of motherhood but to acknowledge the reality that it's a lot harder to raise kids than it is to earn a living. (Men, if you don't think that's true, then you're in a lot more denial than you realize.) It's also possible that the wife had to give up her dreams about where she wanted to live or what kind of work she wanted to do in order to support her husband's education or career. Now that the kids are out of the house and he's no longer tied to the office, she might want to go out and slay her own dragons.

At the same time, he might be a little bit tired from all those years of work. He may want to kick back and take it easy. She might want to move to a location closer to her aging parents so that she can take care of them, while he wants to stay in the house where they've lived for all these fine years. If you don't see trouble brewing, then you better think again. The husband will be feeling vulnerable, and so will the wife.

There is nothing—absolutely nothing—to take the place of couples' counseling at times like these. You've got to get your act together as a couple or you'll end up acting separately. There really isn't a middle ground.

Sometimes couples have the mistaken notion that, now that they're retired, they must do absolutely everything together. This simply isn't true. It's highly unlikely that a couple will find the perfect activity that he loves and she loves. It happens extremely infrequently. A lot of the time, he loves to play golf and she loves to work on her rose garden. She shouldn't be dragging him into the rose garden, and he shouldn't be dragging her off to the first tee. Don't make the other person feel responsible to take on your avocations. That's a setup for disaster. If there are places where your interests overlap, congratulations—take advantage of those commonalities. But you don't have to spend every waking minute together.

Your Brain—Use It or Lose It

Earlier, we said that work provided you with intense intellectual stimulation, for thirty or forty years or more. You were always growing and learning as a professional in your field. *You must find something now to fill that void.* You've got to pick up new ways to challenge yourself intellectually. If you're thinking about moving, consider what adult education opportunities exist in the communities to which you are attracted.

You might have said to yourself, "As soon as I retire, I'm going to read all those books I never had the time to read." After a month or two of steady reading, you're probably going to be climbing the walls, wanting something a little more physical. Here's where I make my plea for balance.

You've got to find a working balance between your intellectual and physical pursuits. The reverse is true as well. You might have said, "As soon as I retire, I'm going to be on the golf course every day!" Well, after you've gotten all that pent-up golf out of your system, what are you going to do now? That's why the idea of finding ways to challenge and stimulate yourself intellectually will put years on your life.

Amy Webb is another psychologist to whom we turn when our clients face these very important issues. She has worked her entire career with high-performing executives all over the world. Her clients frequently tell her that they are scared to death to retire. That's because they're astute enough to see these issues coming. They probably don't know how profound those declarations are.

Don't become a statistic. As with most things in life, preparation is the key. How aware are you of how you "do" change? What is your yearning? What needs to be replaced as you leave what you know? How resilient are you to the unknown? These and other questions are the foundation of the work Amy Webb and some other psychologists we work with help answer.

Staying Together

You've got to keep in mind that the rules are changing in your relationship. In many ways, you can think of the transition to retirement as similar to high school, only without the acne. Your body is changing in surprising (and often uncomfortable) ways. You've got to figure out "what you want to do when you grow up." And if you're like most people, your relationship situation is about to change dramatically, as well.

I want to share with you a few suggestions that can turn contentious, striving couples into happy, thriving couples. I'm not going to tell you not to take some great workshops on marriage or get some counseling, but the wisdom of the ages can be boiled down into these few ideas:

- *Don't hold grudges.* You've got to keep in mind that, as Zig Ziglar says, "Yesterday ended last night." The happiest couples—of any age—don't keep score, don't remember the past (when it's negative), and don't beat each other up over failings, perceived and real.

- *Be fair.* We mentioned earlier that the wife might have sacrificed her choice of where to live so as to support her husband's career. Now it's time for the husband to make a few sacrifices of his own. If she does have aging parents and it's important for her to live near them, then he ought to be willing to pack his bags and be a part of that situation. Marriage isn't about winning or losing. It's often pointed out that a lot more is negotiated in the divorce hearing room than at the marriage altar. You didn't go in keeping score, so make sure you don't do that now.

- *Keep in mind that there is no such thing as a perfect marriage ... or a perfect spouse.* Don't compare your situation to the mythical ideal. No one is happy *all* the time. In fact, you don't have to be happy all the time to live happily ever after. If there are differences that you need to work out, for goodness sake, work them out—and let them go. Your active, happy future depends on it. Dr. Sotile points out even the happy couples have, on average, twelve unresolved issues. What do these couples do that unhappy couples don't do? They express their feelings for each other with brief episodes of care and connection. It's as simple as saying "You look great today" or "You know, such-and-such happened to me today and it reminded me of the time we had so much fun on that trip last fall." These daily uplifts make all the difference in the world. Try it, but be sincere.

Avoiding Depression

The best way to avoid depression is to be a future-based person. Developing your future-based self—thinking about who you want to be and what you want to do in, say, a year to three years from now—is the best way to stave off any kind of depression or negativity.

Also, cut yourself some slack. You're not supposed to have the body of a forty-year-old when you're sixty-five. Look for the good in yourself. I'll bet you don't look too bad for someone that's sixty-five! Squint if you have to. Then focus on what you want the future to look like. Who you are right now is a product of where you've been, not where you're going. Don't have regrets. Since nobody has a time machine, this won't do you any good. If you find yourself mired in thoughts of yesterday, it may be time to discuss these thoughts with a competent therapist or health professional.

Learn from your past, but do things now based on who you want to become. Now that you have time flexibility, you can afford to spend the time to work on whatever you want. If you need help to make this happen, talk with your spouse, therapist, religious leader or a best friend. Just know that you're the only one that can make you feel bad and get strength from that.

Take a Back Seat

By the time people like you retire, they are either at the top of the tree, near it, or they own the whole forest. Now, in retirement, you want to be careful not to assume that you must have a leadership role in anything to which you turn your attention.

For example, let's say you want to get involved with Habitat for Humanity. The hard-charging person you were in your working career would naturally pick up the phone and establish a new chapter in your community, then set to work building 200 houses within the next six months.

Not so fast, partner! When it comes to making commitments of your time, it's best not to charge in. Instead of being the chief and building two hundred homes, why not be one of the rank and file and drive 200 nails? By then, you'll know whether you really want to be involved in Habitat for Humanity for the rest of your life, or whether it was an idea that didn't quite pan out. The same is true for any volunteer—or paid—commitment you may make next. The best advice: Try before you buy.

It is important to get involved socially, to build new networks or to replace the ones that aren't present because you are no longer at work. You need something to retire *to,* not just *from.* But you don't want to get your-self overly caught up in an organization of any kind until you know, through experience, that it's really the place where you want to be.

Moving On?

We talked in earlier chapters about how inertia keeps many retirees anchored to homes and communities that don't offer everything that could be enjoyed at this special time in their lives. I know a Realtor who says that a house is like a living scrapbook. It's hard for people to imagine living anywhere else—until they see the house they are going to move into next. Then their attitude is "How quickly can we sell this thing and move on?" In fact, she says that people who are selling homes and don't know where they're going often put up psychological roadblocks to the sale of those homes and are very difficult clients, indeed.

In retirement, don't let that metaphor apply to you. You've got to know where you're headed and not just where you're coming from. When you've got a sense of destination in mind—something you want to accomplish, a new vision for your life—you are much more likely to avoid the depression, divorce, and early death that happens to retirees who don't make a plan.

Stay Busy

It's ironic—it's often harder for me to get my retired clients to come into the office for appointments than my working clients! We all know the old maxim: If you need something done, give it to a busy person. It's never truer than in retirement. When people have nothing to do, suddenly they have no time in which to get it done. Or they'll go to the opposite extreme and book their schedules so heavily that they've got no time for their financial planning, or for anything else important.

Again, it all comes down to balance. When you're planning your sched-ule, stay busy, but not so busy that you are more jammed now than you were back then. No one's ever written a book called *My Type-A Retirement,* because they never live long enough to write it.

Finally, keep in mind that there's no such thing as a typical retirement. You'll find your niche through trial and error, the same way you figured out how you wanted to live earlier parts of your life. You can do some planning, but at some point you've got to test those plans and see how they work in the real world of your own personal retirement.

One size doesn't fit all. The way Joe down the block is living may not make sense for you. Similarly, don't let your kids, spouse, financial planner, or anyone else tell you *how* you should live the rest of your life. There really are no shoulds, especially now. You've worked hard all your life to create the assets so that you can have this potentially sweetest time of your life to enjoy with your spouse and other loved ones. This is not a time to measure your life in terms of productivity—it's a time to live in a maximum sense of alignment with your values.

As in high school, you get to ask yourself, "Who am I going to be when I grow up?" You can do absolutely anything, so it's important to strike that balance between doing everything and doing nothing. Find the people, the commitments, and the activities that matter the most to you and share them, as appropriate, with your spouse and other loved ones. You now get to live life with a purpose as never before.

Make No Mistake ...

Thanks to medical science, sixty is the new fifty, and seventy-five is the new sixty-five! You'll be living longer and healthier than either your parents or grandparents. So make the most of this beautiful time, and intentionally create the life you deserve. You can find more information about what we call "proactive retirement" at www.proactiveretirement.com.

11

Mistake #1: Choosing the Wrong Advisor

You made it. Now who's going to help you look after it?

A surprisingly great number of people who wouldn't hesitate to bring in an expert for anything from carpentry to getting a will drafted tend to go it alone when managing their financial future. As you can imagine, I'm going to suggest that this is not the best way to go. I can already hear you saying, "C'mon, Steve—of course you're down on financial do-it-yourselfers! Otherwise, people like you wouldn't get paid!"

Well, there is a certain amount of truth to that statement. If everybody did it themselves, then there wouldn't be a need for financial planners. The problem is that when people do it themselves, they tend not to maximize their results. In fact, they may well commit one or more of the mistakes that we've discussed in this book, often to their serious financial detriment. If you're not dealing with someone who sees the whole picture and can help you coordinate it effectively, then you're in that role yourself. You may have a stockbroker to help with investing, and a friend at the country club that sells you insurance, and your golfing buddy that drafted a will for you, but in this scenario you are still the one who has to make sure all these efforts are coordinated and moving you closer to your goals. I'm told by clients that this is why they like to work with our firm. We have the expertise and the experience to help in all these areas and more. Taxes consume a huge amount of our wealth over our working years and again when we die in the form of an estate tax. Keep in mind that tax *preparation* only gets your returns filled out. Tax *planning* keeps money in your pocket and out of the government's.

89

My experience as a CPA for my entire adult life and my career-long focus on tax savings and relevant strategies gives our firm a huge advantage. I'm sure you have a CPA doing your taxes. You know what? I have one do my taxes, too. Again, that's because tax preparation is an entirely different skill set than tax planning. Tax preparers are concerned with compliance with those onerous tax forms. It requires a highly detail-minded orientation. Tax planning requires understanding the big picture and a thorough knowledge of tax laws, not forms. No wonder most CPAs involved in tax return preparation are criticized for their lack of planning ideas. That's not the primary focus of their training and priorities! Remember—you need more than outstanding tax preparation. You need outstanding tax planning as well.

Don't Be Impressed by Big Returns

Frequently when I'm interviewing a possible new client and they don't know what else to ask, they'll inquire about what returns our portfolios generate. Don't get me wrong, having a competitive rate of return on your hard-earned dollars is important. It's just that it isn't the place to start your discussions or your due diligence. You first need to know if the person you're talking with can help you structure your retirement years in a way that makes sense for you. Some questions for you to consider:

Do they seem to be a resource that will help you address the various areas we've identified in this book?

Since no individual can be all things to all people, do they have clients like you that they help?

Do they have a team in place to help in the areas where you need help, either internally at the firm, or externally through strategic relationships?

What will their service cost?

How are they paid?

Does their compensation create any conflicts with delivering the best possible advice—do the fees they may receive from financial services companies color the advice they give?

Once you're comfortable that all these things feel right, then you're ready to talk about how they invest money and what their returns look like. But when you get to this stage, you're not looking for the maximum returns in the good years. You want to see how their approach protects your nest egg when the markets go down. If you pick a manager (or a mutual fund for that matter) based on big returns in bull markets, you really need to know how much risk they took to get that return. There is no free lunch here. The bigger the return, the bigger the risk.

I'll never forget about an investor who attended a talk I gave in Colorado many years ago. I talked all about mutual funds and the positive attributes of using them in a portfolio. One of the participants in the audience half-heard what I was saying and when he got back home to Florida, he picked up the latest issue of *Money* magazine and invested his retirement account in the five best performing funds in the prior year. About nine months later he contacted me about potentially working together. As we were talking about his situation, he told me what he had done and how he was not doing well with the "advice" I gave in my talk.

Here's what he did wrong: *He chased returns.* You see, the five best performing funds for the prior year were all investing in very similar securities. He thought he was diversifying, but in reality he was loading up on what worked best in the prior year. Once he saw the error of his ways, we helped him straighten out the portfolio and really get diversity into it. He had made the error of picking things based upon historically high returns—a big no-no with investments. Fund managers make this same mistake, too. It's okay to ask about track record, but at this stage in your life, you should be all about capital preservation with reasonable growth, not maximum upside returns. Remember from Chapter 4 that losses count more than gains.

Don't Wear Your Emotions on Your Financial Sleeve

Financial investments, when you come right down to it, are purchases. Certainly, they are a lot more complicated than buying a car, but pretty much everything that you encounter in the financial world, from a stock to a bond to a trust to a 401(k), is a product that some entity has brought to the marketplace. And here's the problem: You and I have been trained by hundreds of thousands of commercials and advertisements to make our buying decisions for emotional reasons.

Think about every ad you've ever seen. They're appealing to your emotions—the emotion of fear, the emotion of greed, or the "joy" of one-upping your neighbor down the block. Madison Avenue has convinced all of us to make our decisions for emotional reasons. We then find rationalizations with which to justify those purchases. But almost every purchase we make starts in the heart and not in the head.

How does this relate to investing? Simply put, people make their investment decisions based more on how they feel than on what they know. The study I mention in Chapter 4 of this book—by Dalbar Inc. and Lipper Inc.—illustrates this point. They studied the greatest bull market in the history of investing, the period from 1984 to 2000, during which the average stock fund was up 14 percent a year. Frankly, when the market is up that wildly, *anyone* can make money. You don't need my help or anyone else's, until the inevitable downturn.

But even in Dalbar and Lipper's study, the do-it-yourselfers—the people who put money into and took money out of those very same stock funds that averaged 14 percent a year—made less money. *A lot* less money. In fact, they made just a third, on average, compared to the average mutual fund during that same period. Why? Because generally people don't want their money invested unless the investments are appreciating. The trouble with this philosophy is this: When do you know things are going up in value? You guessed it—after they have gone up. And if the market starts to deteriorate, people tend to sell to "cut their losses short." Know what's going on here? Yep, people are buying high and selling low.

You do this enough over time (sixteen years in the Dalbar study) and you end up with less than one-third of just the average stock mutual fund during that period if you just bought and held on to that investment. Can you just imagine how good your results would be if you didn't use the average investment, but the really good ones?

You know why this is such an emotional experience, don't you? You've spent your lifetime working long hours, taking risks, and doing whatever it took to get you where you are today. People are terrified that if they make the wrong financial move, their lifestyle that they so richly deserve could be at risk. Your money carries with it a tremendous emotional load. But you know what? To a professional like me, your money is just another business decision. I don't have the emotional baggage with your money that you do.

Whenever I look at the business pages, I'm hard-pressed to think why almost any individual would feel that he or she has an edge over the big boys on Wall Street. There was a time, decades ago, when an individual, armed with some good research, could beat the market. It's harder and harder to do that today. Our financial world has gotten so complex that it doesn't pay to venture in alone. And if individuals operating during the greatest bull market of all time left two-thirds of their possible returns on the table, why would anyone think it's easier to get by without the help of a professional in up and down times like these?

Eat Your Greens

When a stock is descending in price, suddenly it feels a lot like spinach. Nobody wants it. Just as nobody wants to eat their spinach, similarly, nobody wants to hang on to stocks that are dropping. A falling stock is a stock we no longer like. So what do we do with things that we don't like? If we are operating based on our emotions, we want to distance ourselves from them and get rid of them as fast as we can.

So we sell. The problem is that they don't ring a bell at the bottom of the market, and they don't ring a bell at the top. As we've seen earlier in this book, you don't have to miss too many up days for any given investment to miss out on all of the rise it will enjoy in a given year. As a result, those emotional decisions to sell stocks after a decline in value often lead to serious losses. Eat your spinach! Don't sell stocks just because you don't "feel good" about them. It's so hard to act dispassionately instead of emotionally about one's own money that the need for a responsible professional is abundantly evident.

I'm convinced that people come to us to help with their portfolios because we have an unemotional, highly disciplined and diversified approach. Your money has a lot of emotional baggage attached to it … in your eyes. Yet that same investment portfolio, in my eyes, is just another business decision. In fact, when I work on my own investments, I have to pretend that I'm looking at a client's portfolio or I'm inclined to make those same mistakes. It's just human nature.

So the question then becomes, whom do you want to work with? And how do you find the right person?

Define Your Goals

Most of us don't go into an auto dealership and say, "Sell me a car." Instead, we go in and say, "I need a four-door sedan with trunk space big enough for four sets of golf clubs." It's up to you to define your goals as you seek to determine whom best to choose as your financial advisor. Do you want someone to manage the whole enchilada, or just a specific part? Perhaps you have concerns about your health as you become older, and you want to make sure that you don't become dependent on your kids. In that case, you need someone who is either a long-term care-insurance specialist, or a financial planner who has access to one. Your first job, before you even start interviewing potential advisors, is to define what you are looking for in the relationship. Just what do you want the person to do?

Alphabet Soup

The marketplace for financial services is a crowded and confusing one. We can begin with the question of what initials to look for after a planner's name. Do you want a CFP? Or a ChFC? If you run into a CPA/PFS, a CLU, a CFA, or a CRPC, should you hire the person, or tell them to CULater?

Some of the designations that follow the names of financial planners, insurance agents, and accountants indicate that you most likely have a person of high ethical standards and professionalism. But how can you be sure? Let's take a quick survey of the "alphabet soup" of initials that follow planners' names.

Back in 1981, when I was leaving the accounting field, it wasn't easy to know which financial-planning designations would stick. Since I lived in Colorado, and the College for Financial Planning was located in Denver, and they promoted the Certified Financial Planner (CFP) designation, that was the one I sought. There were only around 300 CFPs in the United States at that time. As luck would have it, CFP became the dominant designation for financial planners. As of this writing, there are 52,000 CFPs in the United States, with thousands more coming on board each year.

The second most popular designation is ChFC, or Chartered Financial Consultant. This is pretty popular as well—there are currently 41,000 ChFC's. Both of these designations—CFP and ChFC—indicate that an individual is required to take continuing education in financial planning, investments, insurance, and other related fields, and also has to maintain high ethical standards, taking continuing-education courses in ethics as well. If an individual you are considering has either a CFP or a ChFC designation, you have reason to believe that they are the real deal. In my career, though, I've known people with these designations that I wouldn't trust to balance my checkbook and I've also known great financial planners that have no designation. It's not a surefire sign of competence, but at least it shows that someone is serious enough about their career to go out and get the education required. As the field has become more crowded, this is a first screening that should be done.

Without a CLU?

There are other designations that, in my opinion, mean a whole lot less than these first two. For example, many CPAs identify themselves in the marketplace as CPA/PFSs—with the latter letters standing for Personal Financial Specialist. CPAs really know about taxes, as well they should, since taxes are the largest outlays we have when it comes to cash flow. And yet, do CPA's really know the most about your entire investment future?

This isn't usually the case. There are certainly some CPAs who are extremely well versed in financial planning issues, but they are the exception and not the rule. In fact, the PFS designation has never really taken off. For a while, they tried to market the term by telling you that if you were both a CPA and a CFP, and a member of the AICPA, they would automatically give you a PFS! (Still with me?)

I wasn't impressed with the offer and didn't even bother filling in the form, simply because the PFS has no separate continuing education requirement and no ethical component other than the ethical standards of CPAs. So if you see a PFS after an accountant's CPA title, don't be overly impressed. It does mean that this individual knows more about financial planning than the average CPA, but I'm not convinced that they know nearly as much as the average CFP or ChFC. If they don't hold one of these other designations, I'd want to know what types of services they provide. Many will be income tax practitioners that do a little financial planning on the side. I know what that life is like since I used to live it back in the seventies. You get so bogged down with taking care of the income tax that you're not as effective on the financial planning side. For *your* money, you need someone that deals with these issues more than just on a part-time basis.

Then you've got CLUs, or Chartered Life Underwriters. This designation is issued by The American College, and typically CLUs sell life insurance and annuities. Since life insurance and annuities are almost inevitably commission-based products, it stands to reason that such individuals are likely to have a bias in favor of such products. Do you need whole life insurance? Do you need annuities? Let's put it this way: These products are sold more often than people actually need them.

There are certainly some CLUs out there who can do a great job of financial planning—they'll do more than just sell you life insurance, an annuity, and put you in one mutual fund or another—but my question to CLUs is always: Why not become a ChFC as well? The same entity that offers the CLU designation also offers the ChFC designation. When you're trying to find somebody to guide you with your financial planning, you need somebody who doesn't have a commission to gain by putting you into a product that you may or may not need.

All the Way with CFA

A really terrific set of initials to have after your name is CFA, which stands for Chartered Financial Analyst. These three letters are tough to get and require a very high level of investment expertise. The people who run mutual funds, who pick stocks or managers, are CFAs. I'm not a CFA, but John Hageman, a member of our team, is. So we've got all the bases covered. There's also the CIMA designation, which stands for Certified Investment Manager Analyst. These individuals are typically more investment-oriented than CFPs and ChFC's and that designation, in my mind, confers a high level of trust when it comes to investment expertise.

Next, there is a bunch of what I would consider lightweight programs. I consider them lightweight because they lack a continuing education requirement or an ethics component. For example, there is CRPC, a Chartered Retirement Planning Consultant. Again, no continuing-education requirement, no ethics component. I've got this one myself, but I did it for the education, not the initials, so I don't even bother putting it on my business cards. The entities that create these programs come up with these fancy initials so that they can sell their educational programs, some of which take only a weekend to complete. So beware if this is the only designation that someone has.

There's also the RFC, which stands for Registered Financial Consultant. This is the new kid on the block, and there are 6,000 of these. The RFCs have struggled to create trust and credibility, but they do represent a certain standard of integrity.

You might ask why all these groups haven't merged. You might also ask why there are so many heavyweight boxing divisions. The answer is pretty much the same: Everybody wants to control their own piece of the pie. In the year 2000, the National Association of Insurance and Financial Advisors was founded, but the group didn't really work out. It turned out that insurance brokers wanted to sell policies, on which they could make commissions, while financial planners were looking for more objective ways to deliver a service. Sometimes an insurance policy is necessary. That's why we're licensed to shop for these products on your clients' behalf. However, we're aligned with a huge, national insurance brokerage firm where we can secure coverage with any of a multitude of companies. In this way, we can help secure needed policies, but it is a small part of our revenue and we represent our clients, not any insurance company. This helps out clients and we don't have to sell anyone anything to make a living.

The bottom line: Don't be impressed by initials. They're only a starting point to guide you toward—or away from—a given advisor. You should feel free to ask someone what those initials mean after their name. Also do some research on your own—Google is a great resource.

Talk to Strangers

I hope I've somewhat demystified the alphabet soup with which financial planners, insurance brokers, and CPA's seek to impress you. Once you've gotten past that level of inquiry, the next question is whom to meet. I always like to tell people to say no to the "friends and family plan." In other words, don't have your brother-in-law or Bill down the street managing your money. It's just too important. What happens if the investments they choose go south? Now you not only have a financial problem, but you'll also have a family or friendship problem.

I don't want friends as clients. I'm friendly with my clients, but there's no underlying friendship at stake; it's more in the order of a business friendship. I tell most of my non-client friends that I won't let them engage me as their financial planner. It's just best to keep those relationships separate. You can be more objective about relationships that you begin on a business level, and quite frankly, they can be more objective about your investments, as well. So if you're not going to turn your money over to a family or friend (and I could tell you horror stories about people who make that mistake), where do you turn?

Don't Let Your Fingers Do the Walking

Contrary to popular opinion, the Yellow Pages is simply the worst place to find a financial planner. I put my name in there, but I do it as a convenience for people who are looking specifically for me and our firm. You're just as likely to find a financial scammer than a good financial planner. Almost all of my new business comes from referrals. On the rare occasion that I get a "cold call" from an individual who does not come in as a referral, I'll ask how they found me. If they tell me it was through the Yellow Pages strictly on the basis of the listing, I'm shocked. I'll say to them, "Are you crazy? From all you know, I could be a complete crook! So could anybody in the Yellow Pages! I'm happy to talk to you, but don't make this mistake again!"

How many people do you know who have lost some or all of their life savings, due to a simple mistake like this? Answer: More than you realize, because who's going to admit to something as dumb as that?

Here are two proven ways to find quality, ethical, responsible financial planners in your locale. First, talk to friends who have similar financial situations. Get referrals from them, and then meet more than one financial planner. This has to be a good fit, not just professionally but personally. You've got to feel comfortable being totally open and really communicating with this person. It doesn't do you any good if the personality of the financial planner is so authoritarian that you don't feel comfortable saying no to a particular idea. Meet more than one, and keep on meeting them until you find someone with whom you connect.

A second way to find potential financial planners is to visit the website PaladinRegistry.com. This website is, in my opinion, the leading privately owned organization that does "due diligence" on financial advisors. For a financial-planning firm to be recommended as a five-star firm by Paladin, they have to fill out a considerable amount of paperwork and then be rated by Paladin based on longevity in business, ethical behavior, good business practices, and a lack of conflicts in delivering advice.

As a consumer, you can go online, answer a few questions, and get a list of planners in your area that may meet your needs. We pay a monthly fee for being on the registry, but it takes way more than just paying their fees to pass their scrutiny. We consider the few hundred dollars a month that we pay to keep our Paladin Registry listing insignificant compared to the amount of credibility it gives us.

Trust ... but Verify

Anyone who provides investment advice must be registered as a Registered Investment Advisor (or RIA just to add to our alphabet soup) by their state government or by the federal government, depending on the size of their firm. If you have $25 million or more under management (which is not all that large a sum, when you think about it), you must register with the

Securities and Exchange Commission. Investors can visit www.sec.gov, click on Investor Information, move through the document to Investment Advisor Public Disclosure, and then find an Investment Advisor search menu. Here, you can look up any investment advisor in the country, including my own firm. You can see how we're compensated, how much money we have under management, how many disciplinary actions have been filed against us (none, hopefully), and other important information. The SEC is simply looking for full disclosure—they're not testing for quality. But I'll tell you this: You don't lie to the SEC! They can audit and close down any improperly behaving financial advisory firm in a heartbeat.

Keep in mind that Registered Investment Advisors are different from stockbrokers, in that we have a fiduciary responsibility to our clients, a higher level of ethical standards than do stockbrokers. Some stockbrokers are Registered Investment Advisors or affiliated with organizations that are RIAs, but most of the "registered representatives" smiling and dialing, as they say, trying to sell you on the latest hot stock are not. There are good stockbrokers out there, but keep in mind that many still work on a commission basis. And even some of those are able to see beyond the conflict of interest (the more often they buy and sell on your behalf, the more money they make) and actually work for the long-term good of their clients.

Are Commissions Ever Appropriate?

The reality is that sometimes we do get commissions, because there are times when we believe it's important for our clients to have, for example, life insurance or another commission-based product. If there is a commission, there's an inherent conflict of interest. Therefore, we disclose that commission and both of us—our firm and the client—must sign off on it. I don't want our clients to have any surprises.

On the investment side, we don't receive commissions, because there are so many non-commissioned products from which to choose. Some advisors—most notably insurance and annuity salespeople—derive most or all of their earnings from commissions, so naturally they are going to feel more inclined to put you into whole life or an annuity.

Stocks and Bondage

If you're looking for help on the investment side, you want to be extremely careful when choosing the right stockbroker. The biggest distinction to make is whether the individual in question is operating on a commission or fee basis and whether the account is managed on a discretionary or non-discretionary basis. A discretionary account means exactly what it sounds like: The stockbroker has the right to buy and sell without consulting you. With a non-discretionary account, they must consult you before they make any move.

We've all heard the story of the retiree in Florida who gave a stockbroker with a nice Brooks Brothers suit and a great smile a check for $2 million, and is now filing suit against the stockbroker and his firm for churning the account down to $500,000. Don't be that person (the client or the stockbroker). Commission based, discretionary accounts are perfectly legal, but do they make sense? That's only for you to say.

I've been around the financial planning industry for twenty-five years, and as I've shared with you, I worked as a CPA for many years before the financial planning world even came into existence. I started this chapter with the awareness that you might find some of my advice self-serving.

The fact is that most people reading this book ultimately will not choose to work with my firm simply because we are geographically inappropriate or because they're already working with someone they trust. I'm fine with that. I'm simply trying to share with you the benefit of my decades of experience in the financial services field.

When an advisor bases his income strategy on receiving commissions for products, that advisor does not have your best interests at heart. If an advisor is taking a management fee, then you don't have to worry about churning your account—making trades just for the sake of generating commissions—nor do you have to worry about that individual putting you into insurance or annuity products that you really don't need.

When you think about it, the fee-based planner is the individual who really shares your goals. The more your account grows, the more money he or she makes, because their fee is based on a percentage of the account. Such an individual is not beholden to insurance companies and does not have to push a given stock because the higher-ups at their brokerage house are insisting on it. Instead, you have the best chance of getting the dispassionate advice to get you where you want to go.

Make No Mistake …

Who's the best advisor for you? Someone who understands your needs and concerns, someone who comes highly recommended either by a referral source or by an independent body like Paladin, and someone who is primarily fee-based and not primarily or completely commission-based. If you're old enough to remember the Watergate hearings, U.S. Senator Sam Ervin of North Carolina liked to say, "Whose bread I eat, his song I sing." You're a lot better off if you can avoid a mistake of having your financial planner singing out of somebody else's songbook. Instead, find the right person, then go off and make beautiful (and lucrative) financial music together.

12

The Biggest Mistake of All

The biggest mistake of all is to read a book like this and either create a plan and not act on it or to not even create a plan at all. No plan is any good unless it's put into action. The best advice I can offer you is simply this: *Do something.* Go through the table of contents one more time and make a list of the three things that you got out of this book that can change your life the most. Ask yourself these questions:

- What do I need to work on?
- Where do I need help?
- What preconceived notions do I need to reexamine?
- Where do I go from here?

I hope you'll make an action plan, and I hope you'll actually put that plan into effect.

The wise reader will use this book to identify areas that might have been ignored in the past or haven't been considered with all of the necessary information. It's been my goal in this book to help you improve your situation. After all, retirement is supposed to be the sweetest time in your life. It's not just a final chapter in your story—it's an entire sequel to the life you have already lived. Thanks to healthier lifestyles and medical advances, you might just be around for a long, long time! I hope for the best for you in retirement. You worked so hard to climb up the corporate ladder or to build your business. Now that you've worked your way to the top, I'd hate to find you in a position where there's no way to maximize what you have created for yourself.

I guess it's okay to go out and make mistakes that no one else has ever made. That's the road to discovery, the path that the Galileos, Newtons, and Einsteins of the world have taken. But there's really no reason to make a mistake that other people have made, and it's been my purpose in this book to share those critical mistakes that can be extremely difficult from which to recover. Now you don't have to make any of them. You can go out and create an even more satisfying retirement—financially, emotionally, spiritually, and, most of all, in terms of the relationships you get to create, re-create, or improve.

Again, I wish you truly the best. I hope you'll visit my website, www.proactiveretirement.com, to learn the latest with regard to these matters. I look forward to hearing from you, so please contact me anytime at SteveMorton@ProactiveRetirement.com.

May your golden years be the most joyous years of your entire life. And just as in a fairy tale, may you live happily ever after.

978-0-595-45476-1
0-595-45476-3

Printed in the United States
83070LV00004B/301-339/A

9 780595 454761